The Fruits of Victory: Alternatives in Restoring the Union, 1865-1877

THE
FRUITS
OF
VICTORY

Alternatives in
Restoring the Union,
1865-1877

Revised Edition

Michael Les Benedict
Ohio State University

UNIVERSITY
PRESS OF
AMERICA

LANHAM • NEW YORK • LONDON

Library of Congress Cataloging-in-Publication Data

Benedict, Michael Les.
The fruits of victory.

Bibliography: p.
1. Reconstruction. 2. Reconstruction—Sources.
3. United States—Politics and government—1865–1877.
4. United States—Politics and government—1865–1877—
Sources. I. Title.
E668.B462   1986   973.8   86–15789
ISBN 0–8191–5557–8 (pbk. : alk. paper)

All University Press of America books are produced on acid-free
paper which exceeds the minimum standards set by the National
Historical Publications and Records Commission.

To My Mother and Father

Contents ═══════════════

Foreword

"When you judge decisions, you have to judge them in the light of what there was available to do it," noted Secretary of State George C. Marshall to the Senate Committees on the Armed Services and Foreign Relations in May, 1951.[1] In this spirit, each volume in the "America's Alternatives" series examines the past for insights which History—perhaps only History—is peculiarly fitted to offer. In each volume the author seeks to learn why decision makers in crucial public policy or, more rarely, private choice situations adopted a course and rejected others. Within this context of choices, the author may ask what influence then-existing expert opinion, administrative structures, and budgetary factors exerted in shaping decisions? What weights did constitutions or traditions have? What did men hope for or fear? On what information did they base their decisions? Once a decision was made, how was the decision maker able to enforce it? What attitudes prevailed toward nationality, race, region, religion, or sex, and how did these attitudes modify results?

We freely ask such questions of the events of our time. This "America's Alternatives" volume transfers appropriate versions of such queries to the past.

In examining those elements that were a part of a crucial historical decision, the author has refrained from making judgments based upon attitudes, information, or values that were not current at the time the decision was made. Instead, as much as possible, he or she has explored the past in terms of data and prejudices known to persons contemporary to the event.

---

1. U.S., Senate, Hearings Before the Committees on the Armed Services and the Foreign Relations of the United States, *The Military Situation in the Far East*, 82d Cong., 2d sess., part 1, p. 382. Professor Ernest R. May's "Alternatives" volume directed me to this source and quotation.

Nevertheless, the following reconstruction of one of America's major alternative choices speaks implicitly and frequently explicitly to present concerns.

In form, this volume consists of a narrative and analytical historical essay (Part One), within which the author has identified by use of headnotes (i.e., Alternative 1) the choices which he believes were actually before the decision makers with whom he is concerned.

Part Two of this volume contains, in whole or in part, the most appropriate source documents that illustrate the Part One Alternatives. The Part Two documents and Part One essay are keyed for convenient learning use (i.e., references in Part One will direct readers to appropriate Part Two documents). The volume's Part Three offers the user further guidance in the form of a Bibliographic Essay.

Part One

The Fruits of Victory

1

Confederate Self-Reconstruction (Alternative 1)

Winning had been more important than figuring out what to do afterwards. So in April of 1865, when the great rebellion finally collapsed, northern leaders were without an established policy to put the country back together again. Of course, Congress had wrangled off and on during the war about how the Union ought to be "reconstructed." In 1864, Republicans passed a law about it—the Wade-Davis Reconstruction bill, named after its sponsors in the House of Representatives and the Senate. The bill required southerners to frame new state constitutions abolishing slavery, prohibited Confederates from participating in the restoration of state authority, and effectively delayed the whole process until after the war ended. But Lincoln had refused to sign it in the waning days of the Thirty-eighth Congress, because he had other ideas about what to do. After Union troops occupied large chunks of Tennessee, Arkansas, and Louisiana, he urged citizens in those states to "reconstruct" themselves (although behind the scenes he urged Union military commanders in each of the states to use their influence to develop these Reconstruction movements). He offered amnesty to anyone who would swear loyalty to the United States and would agree to recognize the emancipation of former slaves. Then he instructed his military commanders that whenever the number of men taking this so-called amnesty oath in a state equaled one tenth of the votes cast in the 1860 presidential election, they should permit a new state constitutional convention to meet and reorganize civil governments. By the time the Confederates surrendered, such governments had been established in the three states.

But it had taken so much military pressure to accomplish the task, and the newly reborn loyalism seemed so weak that Congress had decided it was not yet safe to recognize the new governments as restored to the Union. And now that the rebels had stopped fighting, even Lincoln wasn't sure what to do. In his last speech, he urged recognition of the three "state" governments already set in motion under his plan, but he and his cabinet were reworking the system for the rest of the southern states.

Southern Fears and Hopes

For the conquered southerners, looking over the wreckage of the land they loved, there was no question as to what sort of reconstruction they preferred.

Their valiant struggle to preserve a way of life other Americans found heinous had led to chaos and destruction. A forty-mile wide swath of Georgia, South Carolina, and North Carolina—from Atlanta east to Savannah and north to Raleigh—lay devastated by William Tecumseh Sherman's foraging army. The ever-ebbing and flowing tides of battle between Washington and Richmond left northern Virginia desolate. Wherever the armies met, they left the burned husks of plantation houses, the charred skeletons of cities, and the torn wreckage of railroad facilities and bridges.

The financial ruin in the South paralleled—even exceeded—the physical destruction. By war's end, over $1.5 billion of Confederate currency was virtually worthless; those people and businesses who counted their assets in it were penniless. Those who had invested in the $700 million worth of rebel government bonds could recover nothing, except in the unlikely case that the triumphant national government would allow the southern states to pay them off; for all practical purposes, the money was gone. In addition, when the Confederacy confiscated northern property in the southern states, it had required southern businessmen to pay debts owned to northerners into the Confederate treasury. Now those debts were reinstated; southerners would have to pay them off once more, this time to the rightful creditors. And finally, all the southern capital invested in slaves was gone; the slaves were free. Crushed by debt, without money to liquidate it or capital to invest, the southern economy lay in ruins.

Worst of all, in ex-Confederates' eyes, the South faced the uncertainties of a social and economic revolution born of the emancipation of its former slaves. Northern observers touring the South after its surrender found that southern whites seemed to think of nothing else. "Everybody talks about the negro, at all hours of the day, and under all circumstances," one of the visitors reported. "One might in truth say--using the elegant language of opposition (racist Democratic) orators in Congress--that the people have got nigger on the brain."[1]

Slavery had been both an economic and social institution. It had arisen out of economic necessity. Southern cash crops--sugar, rice, tobacco, and cotton--required intense labor. Yet from the time English colonists first settled in the South, planters had been unable to secure labor at an acceptable economic and social cost. With so much land available, it had proven impossible to secure a white agricultural labor force. No one could afford to pay workers enough to persuade them to remain agricultural laborers voluntarily. Planters had responded by bringing indentured servants from England--men who had agreed to serve for a term of years in exchange for passage to America and food and shelter. But indentured servants left their masters as soon as their terms of service had expired, if they had not run away before that. Runaway or newly freed servants proved unruly. Planters' efforts to maintain tight controls had led to severe social unrest.

Slavery had been introduced to solve the problem. It provided a disciplined work force at a cost that allowed the production of the South's labor-intensive crops at a profit. The prosperity of the South rested upon this agricultural economy. Land itself was valuable only insofar as cash crops could be raised upon it profitably. Southern bankers, lawyers, transportation companies, artisans--in short, almost everyone but subsistence farmers--depended upon agricultural prosperity for their own livelihoods. Therefore, the economic well-being of nearly all white southerners depended upon the ability to maintain a reasonably priced agricultural work force.

Could such a work force be maintained without coercion? Few white southerners believed that it could. Black slavery was associated with a whole set of social beliefs about black character that made it seem impossible. Blacks were inherently lazy, white southerners insisted. They were unable to plan for the future and therefore unwilling to work any harder than necessary to secure their immediate wants. They had no sense of moral obligation and therefore would not honor labor contracts or feel any loyalty to their employers. Slavery might be gone, southerners believed, but some form of compulsion would have to replace it if the southern economy were to survive. "You Northern people are utterly mistaken in supposing anything could be done with these negroes in a free condition," a South Carolina politician urged one visiting northerner. "They can't be governed except with the whip."[2]

At the same time as it provided a controlled supply of labor, the slavery system had permitted whites to maintain a rigid control over the black population. They were sure that their former slaves were but a step removed from savagery—shiftless, uneducable, capricious, and vicious. Some system of social control would have to replace slavery, white southerners were convinced. (For examples of white southern views about black character and labor, see Document 1.)

The former rebels were faced with economic chaos and afraid of social upheaval. They were convinced that the victorious northerners could not understand the situation. Naturally, they wanted to keep in their own hands as much control as possible over the reconstruction of their society. If they were successful in retaining the reins of government, they might even benefit in some ways from the changes; one Virginian pointed out that with slavery abolished, landowners might no longer have to take care of old slaves who could no longer work. But northern military officers, occupying the South immediately after the Confederate armies' surrender, were forbidding that kind of wholesale expulsion of ex-slaves from their old homes. Cannily, the Virginian told a visitor, "In order for me to reap any benefit from emancipation, the relation between master and man must be made the subject of wise legislation. That matter ought to be left to the States."[3]

So while some southerners resigned themselves to the likelihood that northerners would insist on unpalatable changes in southern institutions, others urged action. "It has been suggested that our wisest course is to do nothing, but to await the development of events," one Virginia leader told a meeting called to discuss the situation. "I do not approve this suggestion. I think we should endeavor . . . to give shape and direction to our own destiny."[4]

Lincoln's Thoughts on Reconstruction

On at least two occasions in early 1865, before all the Confederate commanders had surrendered, Lincoln came close to offering white southerners the kind of control they wanted over their affairs in exchange for peace. Early in February, Lincoln and Secretary of State Seward met with Confederate Vice-President Alexander H. Stephens, Virginia Senator Robert M. T. Hunter, and former United States Supreme Court Justice John A. Campbell, of Alabama, to discuss possible peace terms. Insisting that peace depended on the Confederacy's complete military surrender and the restoration of United States authority throughout the South, Lincoln and Seward agreed that the end of hostilities would restore all of the rights that the Constitution guaranteed to states. It seems clear that Lincoln was promising to recognize the restoration to the Union of those very state governments that had tried to leave it, and to allow them the traditional right of states to regulate nearly all facets of society. He and Seward even hinted that the Emancipation Proclamation, being a war measure only, might be construed to free only those two hundred thousand slaves living in rebel areas conquered by national troops before a peace agreement was reached. But Jefferson Davis's government was not yet ready to give up all hope of independence, and most Confederates knew better than to think slavery would long survive reunion. Lincoln's terms were rejected.

In April, with Confederate resistance collapsing (Lee had already surrendered), Lincoln again seemed to consider leaving the southern state governments intact. Remembering Lincoln's offer of a few months earlier, Judge Campbell suggested that Lincoln permit the fleeing Virginia state legislature to reassemble in Richmond, now occupied by national forces, for the purpose of withdrawing Virginia's military support from the Confederacy. It was unclear just what authority the legislature would have beyond disbanding Virginia's troops, but when Campbell's suggested call for the reassembly was issued, it implied that the legislature would have broad powers—"The matters to be submitted to the Legislature are the restoration of peace to the State of Virginia, and the adjustment of the questions involving life, liberty and property that have arisen in the State as a consequence of war."[5]

It seemed that Lincoln so desired a quick end to the fighting that he was considering the idea of utilizing the rebel state governments to effect a reconstruction. There is no telling how far he was willing to go in allowing former rebels to retain state power in their own hands in exchange for peace. On April 12, with complete victory imminent, he still telegraphed anxiously to commanding general Godfrey Weitzel in Richmond, "Is there any sign of the rebel ·Legislature coming together?"[6] But shocked northerners, including members of his own cabinet, urgently pressed Lincoln to withdraw consent for the meeting. Such dealings with the Confederate governments would inevitably compromise the shaky, loyal governments organized during the war in Arkansas, Tennessee, and Louisiana, as well as the loyal government of Virginia, which the national government had recognized since 1861. As Chief Justice Salmon P. Chase warned the president, he was inviting pressure to recognize the rebel governments in exchange for their mere profession of loyalty. "It will be far easier and wiser, in my judgment, to stand by the loyal organization already recognized," he urged.[7]

When Lincoln saw that the reassembling Virginia Confederate legislature did intend to claim regular governmental powers, he changed his mind about its meeting. Judge Campbell mistakenly "assumes . . . that I have called the insurgent Legislature of Virginia together, as the rightful Legislature of the State . . . ," Lincoln telegraphed Weitzel. "I have done no such thing."[8] To avoid the consequences of the meeting, Lincoln ordered Weitzel not to permit it. Yet, on the very day that he was shot, Lincoln told his cabinet, "We can't undertake to run State Governments in all these Southern States. Their people must do that, though I reckon that, at first, they may do it badly."[9]

The proposals for a restoration of the Union that would consciously leave state power in the hands of ex-rebels culminated in the confusing days after Lincoln's assassination and Vice-President Andrew Johnson's elevation to the presidency. In North Carolina, General Sherman negotiated the surrender of the last major rebel army in the southeast, commanded by General Joseph E. Johnston. Sherman had spent some of the happiest years of his life in Florida and in Charleston, South Carolina, and hoped for minimal change in the southern way of life as a result of the war. Aware that Lincoln had favored lenient terms of Reconstruction, Sherman tried to commit the government to a southern-style restoration. He signed an armistice agreement with Johnston which, in return for the disbandment of southern armies, promised presidential recognition for the Confederate state governments wherever no loyal state governments existed (see Document 2). In states where both loyal and rebel governments claimed authority, the Supreme Court of the United States would decide which was legitimate. The Sherman-Johnston agreement provided amnesty for all rebels "so long as they live in peace and quiet, and abstrain from acts of armed hostility"; guaranteed their right to vote and hold office; and even drew into question the finality of emancipation, protecting southerners in "their rights of person and property, as defined by the Constitution of the United States, and of the States respectively."[10] (The amendment to the Constitution of the United States freeing the slaves had not yet been ratified, and, of course, the constitutions of the southern states recognized the legality of slavery.)

The announcement to the cabinet of the Sherman-Johnston agreement forced a final decision on whether ex-rebels ought to retain control of their political institutions immediately after their surrender (and through them of their social and economic institutions as well). That policy had strong support. Democrats had argued through most of the conflict that the Confederate state organizations were the only legitimate governments in the South, although most Democrats denied that they had the right to secede. In early 1865, Democrats in the Senate helped kill a bill to recognize the restoration of the new, loyal government of Louisiana, reconstructed under Lincoln's authority, arguing that Lincoln's Louisiana government did not represent the people of the state. Many Democrats hoped for a quick restoration of the Union, simply by recognizing the ex-Confederate state governments and seating their representatives in Congress, as though nothing had happened.

But few, if any, members of the so-called Union party (made up of Republicans and Democrats who deserted their party in 1861 to support the war) were willing to let their liberality go this far. Lincoln had decided against it just before he died. His cabinet unanimously and firmly opposed such a course. Even General Sherman's brother, Senator John Sherman of Ohio, wrote him gently, "I think the judgment of unprejudiced men has settled upon the conviction that your terms were too liberal. The recognition of the rebel state organizations, now completely in the hands of the worst men of the South, will not answer."[11]

There can be little doubt that recognition of the southern state governments would have proved the quickest road to reunion or that it would have been the surest way to restore white southerners' good feelings toward the government against which they had rebelled, if that was to be Reconstruction's primary object. But most northerners hoped for sweeter fruits of victory than this from the bitter vine of war they had so painfully nurtured for four years. Of course, they had fought to preserve the Union and the Constitution, but they had fought to restore it on a firmer foundation than the one that had crumbled in 1861. To leave the same men who tried to destroy the Union in control of the South; to make no provisions for southern blacks, who had lain at the heart of the controversy; to leave the door open even to the possible preservation of slavery, seemed to settle nothing. The same people, the same issues that had precipitated the great war would remain. So the new president's cabinet—the same men who served Lincoln—unanimously rejected Sherman's agreement. In fact, in an attempt to discredit the proposal before Democrats could endorse and develop support for it, Secretary of War Edwin M. Stanton attacked its provisions in the newspapers so bitterly that General Sherman, his family, and friends never forgave him. Sherman's friend and superior, General Grant, went to Raleigh to try to soften the blow, and Johnston agreed to a virtually unconditional surrender a few days later.

So died, it seemed, "Confederate Reconstruction." No one could know that it would be revived by, of all people, Andrew Johnson, the president of the United States.

Notes

1. Sidney Andrews, *The South Since the Civil War* . . . (Boston, 1866), p. 22.
2. Ibid., p. 25.
3. New York *Nation*, July 27, 1865.

4. Alexander F. Robertson, *Alexander Hugh Holmes Stuart, 1807-1891: A Biography* (Richmond: William Byrd Press, 1925), p. 412.

5. Edward McPherson, ed., *The Political History of the United States of America During the Period of Reconstruction*, 2d ed. (Washington, D.C., 1875), p. 25.

6. Roy P. Basler, ed., *The Collected Works of Abraham Lincoln*, 9 vols., (New Brunswick, N.J.: Rutgers University Press, 1953), vol. 8, p. 405.

7. Ibid., p. 399.

8. Ibid., pp. 406-407.

9. Frederick W. Seward, *Seward at Washington as Senator and Secretary of State*, 3 vols. (New York, 1891), vol. 3, p. 275.

10. William T. Sherman, *Memoirs of General William T. Sherman*, 2d ed., 2 vols. (New York, 1887), vol. 2, pp. 356-57.

11. John Sherman to W. T. Sherman, May 16, 1865, in *The Sherman Letters: Correspondence Between General and Senator Sherman from 1837 to 1891*, ed. Rachel Sherman Thorndike (New York, 1894), p. 251.

2

Presidential Reconstruction Becomes Confederate Reconstruction (Alternative 2)

Andrew Johnson had been born in North Carolina, emigrating with his impoverished family to Greenville, Tennessee, where he opened a tailor shop and became active in local Democratic politics. Proud representative of hilly eastern Tennessee, where independent white men tilled the grudging soil of small farms, he battled the dominant rich, slaveowning planter element of his own party for years, serving as mayor of Greenville, congressman, and governor of the state, before entering the United States Senate in 1857. In 1861, Johnson was the only southern senator to remain loyal to the Union, fighting a desperate, losing battle to prevent Tennessee's secession. When national troops occupied central Tennessee, Lincoln turned to Johnson to become the area's "military governor," and in 1864 the Union party, trying to demonstrate its broad base, nominated him—a southern ex-Democrat—to be Lincoln's vice-president.

But Johnson remained at heart a Jacksonian. He was devoted to the principles of the extreme wing of Andrew Jackson's Democratic party—its glorification of the common man; its opposition to "privilege" and to big, expensive government; its love of the Union; and its commitment to state rights. He had been willing to use whatever national force was necessary to maintain the nation and Constitution he loved, but the Constitution that he struggled to preserve was one which protected the rights of states, and which minimized the role of the national government in peacetime. With the great war over, he wanted a quick return to old constitutional principles. He had not been willing to let the old, disloyal state organizations simply resume their old places in the Union, but neither did he intend to allow the national government to govern the South indefinitely.

The Expansion of Federal Power

President Johnson's desire to return quickly to "the good old days" was not an isolated sentiment. Throughout the North, Americans shared similar

11

feelings. Although many Americans exulted in the replacement of sectionalism with nationalism during the war, others had been terribly uncomfortable with the changes that the Civil War had brought to their system of government. Before 1861, Americans rarely met a representative of the national government, except at the post office. When they paid taxes, it was nearly always to the state tax collector. If someone threatened or attacked them, Americans turned to their local sheriffs or constables. If they served in military forces, it was probably with the state militia. If businessmen had an argument over a contract, or farmers disputed their boundaries, or an employee sought to abrogate a labor agreement, they brought their disputes to a state court.

The Civil War had changed all that. Suddenly the long arm of the national government could pluck a young farmer from his home and family and put him in uniform. If he resisted, he would be arrested by a federal, military provost marshal and tried before a national, military court. The national government put thousands of men whose loyalty was suspect into prison (only briefly, however), and released them only on condition of loyal behavior. The United States government levied income taxes for the first time, collected by national officers. Tax avoidance was punishable in the *federal* courts. At the same time the national government printed paper money and taxed local banknotes out of existence. It created a national banking system and made it almost impossible for local financial institutions to avoid joining it. At first, local banks were even forced to give up their names when they entered the new system. They were renamed the "First National Bank of———" and so on.

The government in Washington claimed even broader powers in the South. Congress passed laws confiscating rebel property and freeing slaves there. As the war closed, Congress sent to the State legislatures for ratification a constitutional amendment that not only abolished slavery but gave Congress the right to pass laws to carry the change into effect. It created the Freedmen's Bureau—a government institution intended to oversee the transition of millions of slaves to freedom, with power to superintend relations between these millions and their white neighbors. These last laws might not affect northerners directly, but they marked a radical departure from the old constitutional limitations on the central government.

Many northerners had resisted this precipitate growth of the national government even during the war. Some state courts declared the national draft law unconstitutional and issued writs of habeas corpus for people arrested by military authority. Publicists carried out regular "pamphlet wars" over the right of the government to pass a draft law, put people in jail without trial, or free the slaves in the South. The Democratic party ran its candidates on platforms of opposition to all the national government's "usurpations" of power. Even most Republicans disliked what they felt they had to do. As early as 1861 Republican Senator James W. Grimes of Iowa unhappily wrote fellow-Senator Lyman Trumbull, "We are gradually surrendering all the rights of the states . . . and shall soon be incapable of resuming them."[1] Even the most committed Unionists warned against the growing reliance on military institutions instead of civilian government and law.

Committed to traditional interpretations of national power under the Constitution, many Republicans defended their wartime measures from Democratic criticism in such a way as to preserve the old balance of the Constitution. Some of them insisted that during wartime—and *only* during wartime—the powers the Constitution granted to the national government to wage war took precedence over other parts of the Constitution. Others insisted that the operation of the Constitution itself was virtually suspended in a crisis as serious as the Civil War. For example, when Chase, then secretary of the treasury, proposed that the government print paper money without gold or silver to back it and require people to accept it in payment of debts, he admitted that he believed the measure was unconstitutional. "But," he told a critic, "we are in a crisis where the letter of the Constitution must yield to that *salus populi* [i.e., inherent law emanating directly from the spirit of the people], which is the supreme law of States [i.e., governments]."[2]

While either theory justified an almost unlimited use of national power during wartime, both plainly implied that the justification would only be temporary; the dangerous precedents would have no application in peacetime. Republicans hoped that the constitutional crisis would produce little permanent constitutional change, but much-loved constitutional limitations must not prevent victory over those who sought to destroy the nation. With the war over, Republicans wanted to get back to normal as fervently as Democrats. In Congress Grimes insisted, "During the prevalence of the war we drew to ourselves here as the Federal Government powers which had been considered doubtful by all . . . of the statesmen of this country. That time, it seems to me, has ceased and ought to cease. Let us go back to the original condition of things."[3] Throughout the North, Americans echoed Grimes's call. Even those who had advocated the strongest possible action to subdue the rebellion wanted restoration of constitutional limitations on the national government, and a return to state-centered civil law.

Reestablishing State Governments

When Johnson turned to Lincoln's cabinet advisers to learn what Reconstruction plan they had been formulating before the assassination, he learned that Secretary of War Stanton had proposed an occupation scheme. He had suggested appointing provisional governors in the South to maintain order through martial law enforced by the army. At the same time the national government would reestablish its revenue offices, post offices, federal courts, and land offices. Lincoln had liked the idea and told Stanton to redraft the plan with minor changes.

On the day after Lincoln's death, Stanton, House Speaker Schuyler Colfax, Senator Charles Sumner, and a few other congressmen pored over the proposal. What was missing was a method for restoring some kind of local self-government; everyone agreed that military occupation couldn't last forever. So with his friends' help, Stanton modified the duties of the military governors to include organizing elections for constitutional conventions which would alter the state constitutions to conform to the new situation. Once the constitutions were changed, southerners could elect new state officers under them. Then he and his visitors argued over who should be allowed to elect the delegates to the constitutional conventions. After long hours of wrangling, Stanton agreed to propose that all loyal men, *white and black*, be allowed to participate.

On May 9, Johnson took up Stanton's proposal with the whole cabinet, and his advisers agreed unanimously to all but its voting provisions. After a long debate, the cabinet divided evenly on the wisdom of giving newly freed southern blacks this share in their state governments, and Johnson took the matter under consideration.

Johnson was a white southerner, sharing the racial prejudices of most white southerners (in fact, of most Americans, in 1865). Yet he was not adamantly opposed to allowing blacks to vote. Like many unionists, he recognized that their political power might provide a useful counterweight to that of ex-rebels. But he was not as concerned as most northerners proved to be about the humanitarian side of the question. He did not view equal rights for both races in the South as part of the fruits of the Union victory. His commitment to fair play for the ex-slaves did not outweigh his strong feeling as a Jacksonian Democrat that it would be going too far to allow the national government to dictate to the states who should be allowed to vote. If southerners themselves were willing to enfranchise blacks through state action, he would not object. In fact, he privately urged southern leaders to do so voluntarily. But he decided that he could not require such a radical political change as part of the Reconstruction process.

On May 29, 1865, Johnson issued two proclamations which embodied his plan of Reconstruction (*Alternative 2:* see Document 3). The first followed Lincoln's wartime policy of offering amnesty to southerners who would swear allegiance to the government and Constitution of the United States. Only a small number of political and economic leaders were denied that opportunity. They would have to ask Johnson for a presidential pardon directly. The second proclamation outlined the process by which North Carolina could reestablish its state government. In it, Johnson adopted Stanton's plan with only minor modifications, with one critical exception— only whites would be allowed to elect the new constitutional convention. In the next month Johnson issued similar proclamations for all the rebel states except Arkansas, Louisiana, Tennessee, and Virginia, where he recognized the loyal governments Lincoln had established.

By his plan, Johnson hoped not only quickly to restore the Union he loved, but to create in the southern states loyal political parties led by men who had opposed secession in 1861 or who had opposed the Confederate war effort afterwards. Johnson expected these new parties, strengthened by the provisional governors' wise use of patronage, to battle the old, discredited secessionists for control of their states, and to affiliate with the Union party of the North. This policy was most apparent in North Carolina, where Johnson appointed as provisional governor William W. Holden, the leader of the small-farmer, central and hill-country wing of the state Democratic party. Holden had run for governor as a peace candidate in 1864. In Alabama, too, Johnson chose as provisional governor the leader of the peace party, Lewis Parsons, a former Whig. In Texas and Florida he named men who had never sworn any kind of allegiance to the Confederacy—Andrew Jackson Hamilton, of Texas, who had fled his state when it seceded, and William Marvin, of Florida, who had remained in Key West, which was held by Union forces. In South Carolina and Mississippi Johnson chose men who had opposed secession in 1861, although they had grudgingly gone with their states when war came.

But Johnson's political assumptions quickly collapsed. In most of the southern states former rebels quickly forgot old animosities and rallied to the support of their new governors, hoping in this way to retain ultimate power. And in most of the states the new governors quickly succumbed to the Confederate's blandishments, appointing them to office, recommending pardons, and cooperating with them politically against the few die-hard loyalists. Only in North Carolina, Texas, and Tennessee did parties develop, as Johnson expected. In Louisiana Governor J. Madison Wells cooperated with both ex-rebels and so-called conservative Unionists, who had remained loyal during the war, while the two groups battled each other. In the other states, ex-Confederates won monolithic control of the new governments by the end of 1865. But by then, Johnson would not care. The former southern rebels were promising him their political support; northern Democrats were courting him, and Johnson believed that he could fashion a new, overwhelmingly powerful political party by combining these elements with moderate Unionists.

As the southern state constitutional conventions met in the fall of 1865, Johnson made clear what changes he expected them to make and what guarantees he required them to offer in exchange for restoration. These were the fruits Johnson expected from the Union victory. First, the southern conventions had to pronounce the secession ordinances of 1861 null and void. Repeal wasn't enough; southerners had to concede that the ordinances had had no legal effect in the first place. Then, each convention had to amend its state constitution to abolish slavery. Third, the conventions had to repudiate all debts contracted by their states during the rebellion. Finally, either the conventions or the state legislatures to be elected under the new constitutions had to ratify the Thirteenth Amendment to the United States Constitution, which abolished slavery throughout the nation.

Several of the conventions balked at one or another of these requirements, but by December, 1865, when Congress reconvened for the first time since the Confederate surrender, nearly all the former Confederate states had complied with the president's conditions. They had framed new constitutions or amended their old ones, elected new state officials, and sent to Washington representatives and senators who claimed the right to take their seats and thus complete the restoration of the Union. As Congress reopened, Johnson seemed satisfied, although it is likely that he expected Congress to refuse to seat congressmen-elect who could not take the "Test Oath"—that is, swear they never voluntarily aided the rebellion.

Southern ex-Confederates seemed to have gotten their way after all. True, they had been forced to pass some legislation that they did not like. Slavery was gone. But everyone knew that the war had killed it anyway. Nullifying the secession ordinances was galling, but it was merely a symbolic gesture, after all. More degrading was the forced repudiation of the debt contracted during the rebellion. That seemed downright dishonorable, as well as costing southern Confederate bondholders millions of dollars. But the ex-rebels had retained control of their state governments; they retained control over their own destinies. They could channel the war's cataclysmic changes in the South in directions most acceptable to themselves. They began by passing a series of laws to regulate the economic, social, and family lives of the ex-slaves— imposing a permanent second-class citizenship upon them (see Document 4). Especially, they placed nearly insuperable obstacles in the way of blacks who hoped to be something other than landless farm laborers. Still convinced that blacks would not work unless they were forced to, they gave the state authorities the power to punish ex-slaves who violated labor contracts and to treat as "vagrants" those would could not find work at all (and implicitly this meant work as a laborer for a white employer; an ex-slave would have a hard time proving to a white sheriff or judge that he was self-employed). "Three fourths of the people assume that the negro will not labor except on compulsion," wrote a northern correspondent in the South, "and the whole struggle between the whites on the one hand and the blacks on the other hand is a struggle for and against compulsion."[4] In this struggle, the whites, thanks to Andrew Johnson, had control of the ultimate weapon—the southern governments.

The question now was, would northerners—specifically their representatives in Congress—permit them to use it?

Notes

1. Grimes to Trumbull, Oct. 14, 1861, Trumbull Mss., Library of Congress, Washington, D.C.

2. James C. Welling to George Bancroft, July 29, 1878, Bancroft Mss., Massachusetts Historical Society, Boston, Mass.; John A. Bingham in *Congressional Globe*, 40th cong., 3d sess., Jan. 29, 1869, p. 722.

3. *Congressional Globe*, 39th cong., 1st sess., May 8, 1866, p. 2446.

4. Sidney Andrews, *The South Since the Civil War* . . . (Boston, 1866), p. 398.

3

The Republican Alternatives in 1866: Internal Reconstruction (Alternative 3) or National Protection (Alternative 4)

In later years, many Americans came to believe that President Johnson's Reconstruction plan was a great opportunity lost. Even John Sherman, one of the Republican leaders who finally rejected it in 1866, conceded in his memoirs, "After this long lapse of time I am convinced that Mr. Johnson's scheme of reorganization was wise and judicious."[1] After 1900, and until the 1950s at least, most American historians agreed. In the opinion of those who believed, like Johnson, that the most important goal of Reconstruction was to restore good feeling between northerners and southern whites, acceptance of the presidential plan promised to reconcile conquered Confederates to their defeat.

At the same time, acceptance of the presidential Reconstruction policy by northerners meant that quick return to normal life for which Americans had been hoping. It would mark the end not only of four years of war but presumably of at least twenty years of intense sectional controversy over slavery. Having won freedom for the slaves, Americans would let black and white southerners work out their own adjustment to the change. Naturally, this meant giving white southerners the real say in the matter, but most northerners believed in the racial inferiority of blacks as completely as southerners, and to many of them it seemed logical to leave the question to better-educated, more cultivated people who had to live with the problem. Any other solution, especially one imposed from outside, could only lead to terrible strife in the South. With their strong convictions about black laziness, immorality, viciousness, and brutality, southerners would not acquiesce in anything less than complete white superiority.

A southerner himself, Johnson understood the depth of white southerners' feelings—in fact, shared them. To enforce equality would create "a contest

17

between the races, which if persisted in will result in the extermination of one or the other," he told Frederick Douglass and other blacks who were petitioning him to endorse equal suffrage. "The query comes up right there, whether we don't commence a war of races. I think I understand this thing, and especially is this the case when you force it upon a people without their consent."[2] Johnson's words proved prescient. Republicans' efforts to force black political and legal equality on the South led to massive resistance and even a sort of guerilla warfare, which continued until the attempt was given up.

The Republican Dilemma

For Republican leaders, there were additional, political reasons for endorsing Johnson's policy. In 1865, Republicans still were a sectional party, with almost their entire power concentrated in the North. If they accepted the restoration of the Johnson-created southern state governments, they might win the following they needed among the white people of the South. The provisional governors had established nascent Unionist organizations in Tennessee, North Carolina, and Texas, which would certainly affiliate with the Republican party if properly encouraged. Even though ex-rebels supported the provisional governors in the other ex-Confederate states, those leaders might sustain the Republican party if it proved that it was not antisouthern. (In fact, several provisional governors—Marvin of Florida, Wells of Louisiana, Orr of South Carolina, and Pierpont of Virginia—eventually joined the Republicans, but by then the party was thoroughly disliked by the vast majority of southern whites.) If Republicans in Congress recognized the restoration of the southern states to the Union, rejecting the credentials only of those who had voluntarily supported the rebellion, local Republican parties might make real inroads there. They could urge southern whites to send to Congress only men who could take the Test Oath, and they could appeal to them on economic issues, advocating liberal use of state power to develop the economy, transportation and communication facilities, and educational institutions. Perhaps they might even try to win basic civil rights for the ex-slaves, if it did not cost too many votes.

This course could win advantages in the North too. Republicans would have the credit for winning the war and restoring the Union quickly, with a minimum of friction. At last a national party, they would stand behind a popular, peace-making president, whose policy even Democrats had endorsed. Most important, an endorsement of Johnson's Reconstruction program would eliminate the danger that the president and his conservative Republican followers might leave the party if it were rejected. Such an exodus would be politically disastrous. It would mean that Republicans, instead of expanding their appeal, would face the combined forces of southern ex-Confederates, northern Democrats, and dissident Republicans led by the president of the United States. They could hardly hope to overcome such overwhelming opposition.

But despite the apparent political and social benefits of accepting Johnson's policy, most Republicans decided that they could not endorse it without at least some important modifications or additions. For many, it was a fundamentally moral question. Many Republicans credited the infusion of black soldiers (nearly two-hundred thousand of them) into the armed forces after 1862 with saving the Union. They enlisted knowing that capture meant return to slavery at best, and likely a brutal death. To deny them the basic rights of citizens of the nation they served seemed the rankest ingratitude. Some Republicans regarded the war itself as a sort of divine retribution for Americans' past willingness to sacrifice the slaves' human rights. Even Lincoln, no believer in orthodox religion, had suggested God had given "to both North and South, this terrible war, as the woe due to those by whom the offence [of slavery] came."[3]

As if touched by fire, Minnesota Republican Representative William Windom castigated his own section for trying so long to maintain national harmony at the expense of black men's human rights, or as another abolitionist put it, to "cement the Union with the blood of the negro":

All remember how unwilling we were to do anything which would inure to the benefit of the negro. I recall with shame the fact that when five years ago [in 1861] the so-called Democracy . . . were . . . plotting the destruction of the Government, and we were asked to appease them by sacrificing the negro, two thirds of both Houses voted to rivet his chains upon him so long as the Republic should endure. A widening chasm yawned between the free and slave states, and we looked wildly around for that wherewith it might be closed. In our extremity we seized upon the negro, bound and helpless, and tried to cast him in. But an overruling Providence heard the cries of the oppressed and hurled his oppressors into that chasm by hundreds of thousands until the whole land was filled with mourning—yet still the chasm yawned. In our anguish and terror we felt that the whole nation would be speedily ingulfed in one common ruin. It was then that the great emancipator and savior of his country, Abraham Lincoln, saw the danger and the remedy, and seizing four million bloody shackles he wrenched them from their victims, and standing with these broken manacles in his hands upraised toward heaven, he invoked the blessing of the God of the oppressed, and cast them into the fiery chasm. That offering was accepted and the chasm closed.[4]

To men like Windom, who loosely labeled themselves "radicals," the Republican party was more than a mere political organization; it was the embodiment of the moral crusade against slavery and the fundamental principle of human equality that underlay it. As Senator Samuel C. Pomeroy insisted, "The strength of the Republican party consists in its adherence to principle, and to that embodiment of its principles, equality of rights among men. Without that . . . there would be no motive to sustain the party, and the party would not be worth sustaining. It is, to my mind, all that makes it valuable."[5] As far as these Republicans were concerned, there was no way to rationalize the surrender of principle inherent in the president's policy; no political advantage could justify leaving the former slaves helpless in the clutches of their former masters, embittered by four years of war.

But even if some Republican leaders could exclude moral considerations, and few could, it was not at all certain that the advantages of endorsing President Johnson's policy outweighed the risks. First of all, there was no guarantee that enough white southerners would ever sustain a southern Republican party to make it viable. No matter how lenient its Reconstruction policy might be, the Republican party would always be the party that destroyed slavery, the party that southerners blamed for the suffering of the Civil War.

Second, many Republicans suspected that acceptance of Johnson's Reconstruction policy might weaken rather than strengthen the party in the North. Certainly, it would not long command the loyalty of those committed primarily to its moral principles. As Congressman Josiah Grinnell warned, "Yielding a principle and refusing to demand impartial justice through fear, [the Republican party] becomes occupied with sordid plans, disgusts the moralist, and dampens the ardor of the young and heroic whose service has been determined by the nature of our boldness, constancy, and trust in the Almighty Ruler."[6] Acceptance of the president's plan might also alienate northerners who, while not concerned about black people's rights at all, did not want to see the very Confederates who had tried to destroy the nation continued in power in the South. And finally, if Republicans joined Democrats in endorsing the president's policy, then Civil War and Reconstruction issues would no longer be the most important political questions before the people. This was dangerous, because despite the risk of alienating the president, Republicans were still far more united on questions of black people's rights and Reconstruction than they were on any other question; on other issues—tariff reform, financial reform, and government aid to business, for example—they were hopelessly divided. Did they dare to permit these questions to come to the fore by giving up the issue upon which the party was founded?

So when Congress met in December of 1865, anxious Republican leaders faced the probability of a division in the party whether they accepted their president's policy or rejected it. In one case they would lose Republicans who would not surrender the party's fundamental principles; in the other, they would lose the president, his patronage, and his supporters.

Radical and Nonradical Terms of Peace

Many of the most radical Republicans were willing to let the president go over to the Democrats rather than conciliate him. Men like Senators Charles Sumner, Zachariah Chandler, and Benjamin F. Wade and Representatives Thaddeus Stevens, James M. Ashley, George S. Boutwell, William D. Kelley, and George W. Julian believed that the war had originated in the vast differences between the sections. "Heretofore Southern society has had more of the features of aristocracy than democracy," Stevens insisted. "The Southern States have been despotisms."[7] The nation's future security required fundamental changes in the economic, political, and social institutions *within* the southern states, the radicals argued. For them, a permanent, internal Reconstruction of the South was the key to a firm Reconstruction of the Union (*Alternative 3:* see Document 5). The most obvious change, and the least the radicals would accept, was the political one—enfranchisement of Union-loving former slaves. But radicals knew that even this, the most elemental part of their program, would take time. Julian remembered that "they saw that States must grow, and could not be suddenly constructed where materials were wanting."[8] The best way to proceed, Julian and other radicals urged, was to put the southern states under a long-term "probationary training, looking to their restoration when they would prove their fitness for civil government and independent states."[9] They wanted to sweep away the governments Johnson had created and replace them with territorial governments, like those that governed New Mexico or Montana. The southern "territories" would have their own territorial legislatures, elected by blacks and white alike. Perhaps they could elect their own governors and judges too, or have these officials appointed by the president, as in other United States territories. The territorial governments could make all their own laws, but Congress would retain ultimate authority to step in and revise them or pass new ones if necessary. "I know of no better place nor better occasion for the conquered rebels . . . to practice justice to all men, and accustom themselves to make and to obey equal laws," Stevens explained.[10] The territories would be a classroom, where southern blacks would learn the responsibilities of equality and southern whites would learn to accept it. To aid in the lesson, many radicals urged that southerners be required to organize free public school systems like the ones in northern states so that new generations of southerners would be educated in the egalitarian principles of American republicanism.

Finally, there were those radicals who urged confiscation of large southern landholdings as punishment for the rebellion, and redistribution of the land in small parcels to poor whites and blacks. Not only would this guarantee the permanence of black freedom, but it would assure democracy for blacks and whites alike. As Stevens stated flatly, "It is impossible that any practical equality of rights can exist where a few thousand men monopolize the whole landed property."[11]

But less radical Republican leaders, even many who agreed with the radical program in the abstract, especially its insistence on black voting rights, rejected these proposals. Republican adherence to principle would secure nothing if it alienated the president and conservative Republican voters and swept the Democrats into power, they insisted. More moderate leaders urged, "*Do not let the power pass away.* If necessary let [black] suffrage go, & confiscation also if thereby you can save the rest. . . . If our friends do not unite, Johnson, the Copperheads & the rebels will in the end do the work for you."[12] Since both acceptance and rejection of Johnson's policy promised to alienate large numbers of Republicans and destroy the party, these Republicans decided that the only hope was to do neither. Nonradicals like Senators William Pitt Fessenden, James W. Grimes, and Lyman Trumbull and

Representatives John A. Bingham, Nathaniel P. Banks, and James G. Blaine would accept Johnson's basic policy of leaving white southerners in control of their states, rejecting radical pleas for fundamental change in southern society. But they were not willing to leave the freedmen completely at the mercy of ex-Confederates; they would add to Johnson's policy a program of *national* protection for southern loyalists' basic rights. The problem was, what exactly ought to be added to the presidential program? And given Americans' desire to preserve the old federal system, how could Congress secure these additions without a radical expansion of national power?

It was a tribute to Americans' reverence for their Constitution that the second problem was knottier than the first, for there already was a wide consensus among less radical Republicans about what *ought* to be done, if a way could be found to do it. Deciding that it would be impossible to enforce equal suffrage without losing President Johnson to the opposition, these Republicans agreed that before Congress could recognize the restoration of Johnson's southern state governments, it would have to pass legislation guaranteeing the freedmen equal civil rights, counteracting the restrictive "black codes" being passed in the southern states (see Document 4). By "civil rights" they meant that blacks should have the same property rights, the same individual freedoms, and the same physical security as whites, and equal access to the courts that enforced those rights. Congress would also have to make certain that money borrowed by the national government to finance the war would be repaid and that money borrowed by the Confederate states would not. The best way to do that, Republicans determined, would be to incorporate the requirement into another amendment to the Constitution (*Alternative 4:* see Document 6).

Finally, moderate and conservative Republicans demanded a constitutional amendment changing the way seats were apportioned in the House of Representatives. Under the Constitution as it stood, congressional seats were divided according to population, with free people counting more heavily than slaves. With emancipation, southern states actually stood to gain representation. Republicans insisted that if blacks were not to be permitted to vote, they should not be counted in deciding how many representatives each state would have in Congress; seats should be divided according to how many voters each state had. These requirements, in addition to those the president had already imposed—ratification of the Thirteenth Amendment, nullification of the secession ordinances, and repudiation of the rebel debt—were the minimum peace terms that even conservative Republicans would accept.

Most Republicans hoped to obtain these "fruits of victory" without a fundamental alteration in the federal system. Of course, not all agreed. Some radicals, like Charles Sumner, insisted that if Congress intended to settle for less than major changes within the southern states, at least it should retain some permanent power to protect loyalists there. These radicals found a constitutional justification for such power in the clause of the Constitution that obligated the national government to guarantee each state a republican form of government. That left it to Congress to decide just what constituted republicanism, Sumner insisted, and if at any time a state fell short of Congress's standard, it could intervene.

But Sumner made few converts. Instead, most Republicans turned to a theory offered most persuasively by Richard Henry Dana, an influential Boston Republican lawyer (see Document 7). Building on the widespread notion that the national government held temporarily expanded power during wartime, Dana suggested that it was up to the government to decide when the war ended. In that case the government could demand that the rebel states meet certain conditions in return for the government's recognition that peace was restored. Until then Congress retained its wartime power and could administer the South under it. As Dana put it: "The conquering party may hold the other in the grasp of war until it has secured whatever it has a right to acquire."[13]

One great virtue of this "grasp of war" theory was that it promised only temporary expansion of national power; once southerners met the conditions Congress set, there would be a return to peace and peacetime constitutional limitations. Another was that it seemed to complement the president's policy so nicely. He too had insisted that southerners meet certain conditions before he would recognize their renewed right to self-government. The old Jacksonian Democrat would certainly reject a constitutional argument like Sumner's, which would permanently expand national power, but how could he deny Congress's right to proceed on the same policy he had followed?

The Nonradical Program—and Johnson's Response

As Congress convened, Republican conservatives and moderates began to implement their program. They postponed the seating of southern congressmen and appointed a Joint Committee on Reconstruction made up of fifteen representatives and senators and chaired by the eminent, conservative Republican leader of the Senate, William Pitt Fessenden of Maine. This committee would consider the status of the southern states and suggest what further conditions they would have to meet before Congress would recognize their restoration. Meanwhile, Republicans deflected a radical attempt to provide an opening wedge for black suffrage, by burying in a Senate committee a proposal to enfranchise black men in Washington, D.C. (The bill had passed the House of Representatives after a hard fight.) Instead Republicans turned to two bills designed to protect freedmen from ex-Confederate oppression, sponsored by a very conservative Republican Senator, Lyman Trumbull of Illinois.

The first, the Freedmen's Bureau bill, extended the life of a military department organized during the war to oversee the adjustment from slave to free labor in the South. The bureau supervised the drawing of labor contracts between former slaves and employers, explaining their meaning to black workers; investigated complaints of mistreatment or shoddy work; protected black people where local authorities refused; provided educational facilities; and distributed food, clothing, blankets, and seeds to poor blacks and whites alike. Its continuation was a clear exercise of Congress's temporary war powers (*Alternative 4:* see Document 8).

Trumbull's second measure, the Civil Rights bill, defined American citizenship for the first time, conceding it to "all persons born in the United States and not subject to any foreign power, excluding Indians, not taxed." The bill went on to prohibit discrimination among citizens in property and personal rights, "any law, statute, ordinance, regulation, or custom, to the contrary notwithstanding."[14] Then, in provisions which seemed to contradict Republicans' wish to preserve the old balance of federalism, Trumbull's bill permitted citizens to transfer cases to the federal courts from any state court that continued to discriminate in these rights. The Civil Rights bill seemed radically to expand the jurisdiction of the national government in areas that had always been left to the states. Under its terms, federal courts might soon have been deciding ordinary criminal cases, cases involving contracts, trespasses—in fact, any case from a state which discriminated among citizens in the courts.

Naturally, many Republicans hesitated to endorse such a measure, but they soon learned that Trumbull, who was more committed to state rights than most of them, had devised an ingenious way to *preserve* state jurisdiction at the same time that he forced the states to grant all citizens legal equality. The key was in the provisions allowing citizens who were discriminated against to switch their cases from state to federal courts. After all, if the states lost jurisdiction over these cases, what was the point of retaining the discriminatory laws? Every time a state tried to enforce the discriminations, the case would be transferred to the national courts. It would not be long before states dropped their useless unequal laws. Once they did, citizens would no longer be able to switch cases into the federal courts; the states would get back their old areas of jurisdiction and the national courts would once again be limited to their old business. As Trumbull explained, "[The bill] will have no operation in any state where the laws are equal, where all persons have the same civil rights without regard to color or race."[15] In the final analysis, the Civil Rights bill was designed merely to force states to enforce rights equally, not to protect rights by direct national action.

Although Trumbull's argument helped to reassure his nervous Republican colleagues about his bill, they still were not completely comfortable with it. But for the vast majority of them, the political and moral necessity to find some way to protect the freedmen outweighed any continuing doubts. Republicans passed both the Freedmen's Bureau bill and the Civil Rights bill almost unanimously.

At the same time, the Reconstruction committee worked on constitutional amendments that southern states would have to ratify in order to get out of the "grasp of war." One was the amendment Republican moderates and conservatives wanted—to change the way congressional seats were apportioned to the states. Another guaranteed repayment of the national debt and repudiated the rebel debt. But before the committee could complete its work,

President Johnson shocked the nonradical Republicans by rejecting their program.

Rumors of Johnson's dissatisfaction had been circulating ever since the Republicans had refused to seat southern congressmen-elect who could take the required loyalty oaths. As December, 1865 and January, 1866 wore into February, the president became increasingly impatient. But conservative and moderate Republicans still expected him to forbear a while longer before splitting the party that had elected him to the vice-presidency. Once the Freedmen's Bureau and Civil Rights bills were passed, many Republicans, including Trumbull, felt it would be safe to restore at least some of the ex-Confederate states to their places in the Union, particularly Tennessee and Arkansas.

But Johnson felt that he had waited long enough. Fervently committed to a quick return to the old federal Union, he shared the concern of the influential lawyer and jurist, Isaac F. Redfield, who worried that while the doctrine of state rights had so weakened the national government before the war as to finally threaten its continued existence, "the great danger now will be that things will rush in the opposite direction, and the central authority, from being limited and straightened in all its powers and functions, . . . will be in danger of absorbing all the important functions of governmental administration." [16]

The delay in restoration, the passage of the Freedmen's Bureau bill, the impending passage of the Civil Rights bill, and the radicals' continuing demand that Congress require black enfranchisement in the South convinced Johnson that the critical moment had arrived. Trumbull's argument that the bills would not radically change the federal system did not impress him. Assured of Democratic political support, Johnson was certain that many conservative Republicans would follow him into a coalition whose combined strength would surely sweep the congressional elections in a few months. Confident that he would emerge victorious in any confrontation, Johnson was in no mood to compromise his principles.

The Freedmen's Bureau bill proposed the very extension of power Johnson feared (see Document 9). "The bill will . . . , when put into operation, practically transfer the entire care, support, and control of four millions of emancipated slaves to agents, overseers, or task-masters, who, appointed at Washington, are to be located in every county and parish throughout the United States containing freedmen and refugees," he marvelled. [17] All those agents, appointed under the president's patronage (that is, the custom of appointing people to government jobs as a reward for political service) might create a tremendous political machine. Worse, that machine would control the action of the poverty-stricken people who depended on it; they might not yet have the vote, but Johnson worried that they could be mobilized in other, more ominous ways.

The Civil Rights bill aroused the same concern over "centralization." "In all our history, in all our experience as a people, living under federal and State law, no such system as that contemplated by the details of this bill has ever before been proposed or adopted," Johnson insisted. It marked "an absorption and assumption of power by the General Government which . . . must sap and destroy our federative system of limited powers . . . . It is another step, or rather stride, towards centralization, and the concentration of all legislative powers in the national Government." [18]

At the same time, the president revealed a more vocal hostility to blacks than he had before. Ignoring the simple fact that the freed people had been born in the United States, he complained that the Civil Rights bill discriminated in their favor by making them citizens while immigrants had to wait five years for the same privilege; he insisted that a similar bill might nullify laws prohibiting interracial intermarriage. "In fact," Johnson concluded, "the distinction of race and color is, by the bill, made to operate in favor of the colored against the white race." [19]

Finally, Johnson seemed to deny that Congress had any right to refuse to recognize the restoration of the southern states to their old places in the Union. He would explain this more fully later: the southern *states* had never left the Union; their *officials* had rebelled and therefore the states had been left without legitimate governments during the war. After the North's victory, it was up to the president, as commander in chief of the armed forces, to get the machinery of government in the South moving again. This he had already done, and now the insurrectionary states were again entitled to all their rights under the Constitution. All Congress could constitutionally do was to make sure that individual southern senators and representatives could take the "ironclad" Test Oath that they had never voluntarily aided or abetted the rebellion.

Resolutely, Johnson vetoed both bills.

Republican Conditions of Restoration:
The Fourteenth Amendment

For conservative and moderate Republicans, the worst had happened. Their attempt both to satisfy the president and sustain the moral principles of the party had failed. Once again, they faced difficult choices. They could, of course, wheel into line behind Johnson, avoiding at all hazards the loss of the president to the opposition. But word from local leaders indicated that this course would alienate large segments of the party rank and file; not only radicals would complain.

With little or no political advantage to be gained by abandoning principle, Republican leaders remained firm. "We must hold on, and make an issue upon which we can go to the country," Fessenden wrote an influential Maine Republican. "I do not intend to yield the fruits of the war, unless the people overrule me—and I don't think they will." [20] But conservative and moderate Republicans were still unwilling to follow the radicals' advice and strike out at last for black suffrage, territorialization, and other elements of the radical program. They felt that they dared not risk the defection of the large number of wavering conservative Republicans who did not want to abandon their party for Johnson's coalition with the Democrats. Republicans knew that most of these conservatives wanted to secure a firm Reconstruction and sincerely hoped for guarantees for the rights of the ex-slaves, but they also knew that they would not sustain a radical policy. What was important now was to maintain the unity of the party. Republicans could not spare the conservatives any more than they could the radicals.

So, despite the protests of some of the more uncompromising radicals, Republicans decided to press ahead with the same moderate policy that they had originally designed to conciliate Johnson, even though the president had deserted them. They passed the Civil Rights bill over Johnson's veto, passed a revised Freedmen's Bureau bill, and then proposed to the southern states the conditions that they would have to meet in return for restoration to their old places in the Union.

These conditions were embodied in a new amendment to the Constitution proposed by the Reconstruction committee created at the beginning of the session (see Document 10). The committee's report made it clear that the southern states would have to ratify the amendment before they could be restored to normal relations in the Union. In fact, the committee recommended that Congress pass a bill to make this plain and binding.

The guarantees secured in the proposed Fourteenth Amendment to the Constitution were those that the conservative and moderate Republicans had favored since the beginning of the congressional session. The amendment's first section required states to extend equal rights to all citizens of the United States regardless of race; the second based representation in Congress on the voting population of each state; the third disqualified Confederates who had held state or national office before joining the rebellion from holding office again unless Congress removed the disability by a two-thirds vote; the fourth guaranteed the national debt and repudiated debts contracted by the rebel governments; and the fifth affirmed Congress's power to enforce the others.

Radicals joined nonradicals in the nearly unanimous Republican passage of the Fourteenth Amendment, even though it fell far short of what the radicals had originally wanted. But they dug in their heels when it came to passing the committee's Reconstruction bill guaranteeing the restoration of the southern states after they ratified it. Conservatives and moderates argued that Republicans had to offer a complete Reconstruction program to the voters in order to win the upcoming congressional elections; if they failed to promise that this was the final settlement, enough conservatives might defect to swing the elections to the Johnson-Democratic coalition.

But radicals did not want to foreclose the possibility that at least some parts of their program might be adopted. They still feared that the national government's guarantees of the debt and of loyalty among government officials, and its hesitant promise to protect the freedmen would prove ineffective. "It will prove in the end impracticable to secure to men of color civil rights unless [they] ... are fortified by the political right of voting," Boutwell insisted. "With the right of voting everything that a man ought to have or enjoy of civil rights comes to him. Without the right to vote he is secure in nothing."[21] So radicals still hoped for a restructuring of power *within* the southern states. They fought off the nonradicals' effort to tie Congress's hands.

But when Tennessee ratified the constitutional amendment in July, 1866, just before Congress adjourned, Republicans quickly passed a resolution recognizing her restoration to the Union, easily overcoming a last, futile attempt by radicals to require the state first to enfranchise its blacks. It was a clear signal to the South and to the American people that the Republican policy was complete. In the fall elections, the voters of the North would choose between the president's policy of immediate restoration with no further conditions, or Congress's promise of restoration upon the ratification of the Fourteenth Amendment—the same choices Republicans had faced during the previous session of Congress. Johnson and the Democrats insisted that the Republican policy marked a radical departure from the principles of the American Constitution. They threw in large doses of outright racial prejudice and charged that the Republicans intended to enfranchise the freedmen. Republicans appealed to a volatile mixture of principled concern for black men's rights and continuing fear of renewed southern disloyalty. Again and again they emphasized the moderation of their policy, its rejection of radical alternatives, and urged audiences to weigh the limited extension of national power that they proposed against their desire to firmly secure the fruits of victory.

In the end, most northern voters made the same decision as their Republican representatives, endorsing the Republican policy with an overwhelming victory at the polls. Now all that remained to settle the war issues was for white southerners to ratify the constitutional amendment.

Notes

1. John Sherman, *Recollections of Forty Years in the House, Senate, and Cabinet: An Autobiography*, 2 vols. (New York, 1895), vol. 1, p. 361.

2. Edward McPherson, ed., *The Political History of the United States of America During . . . Reconstruction*, 2d ed. (Washington, D.C., 1875), pp. 53-54.

3. Roy P. Basler, ed., *The Collected Works of Abraham Lincoln*, 9 vols. (New Brunswick, N.J.: Rutgers University Press, 1953), vol. 8, p. 333.

4. *Congressional Globe*, 39th Cong., 1st sess., Mar. 2, 1866, p. 1159.

5. Ibid., 40th Cong., 3d sess., Jan. 29, 1866, p. 708.

6. Ibid., 39th Cong., 2d sess., Jan. 4, 1867, p. 287.

7. Stevens, *Reconstruction: Speech of the Thaddeus Hon. Stevens, Delivered in the City of Lancaster, September 7, 1865* (Lancaster, Pa., 1865), p. 7.

8. George W. Julian, *Political Recollections, 1840-1872* (Chicago, 1884), p. 305.

9. Ibid.

10. *Congressional Globe*, 39th Cong., 1st sess., Dec. 18, 1865, p. 74.

11. Stevens, *Reconstruction*, p. 7.

12. Alexander K. McClure to Thaddeus Stevens, Jan. 13, 1866. Stevens Mss., Library of Congress, Washington, D.C.

13. Richard Henry Dana, Jr., *Speeches in Stirring Times and Letters to a Son*, ed. Richard Henry Dana III (Boston and New York: Houghton Mifflin Co., 1910), p. 246.

14. U.S., *Statutes at Large*, vol. 14, p. 27.

15. *Congressional Globe*, 39th Cong., 1st sess., Jan. 29, 1866, p. 476.
16. Isaac F. Redfield, "Proper Limits Between State and National Legislation," *Albany Law Register*, new series, vol. 6 (February, 1867), p. 197.
17. James D. Richardson, comp., *A Compilation of the Messages and Papers of the Presidents . . .* , 20 vols. (New York, 1897), vol. 8, p. 3601.
18. Ibid., pp. 3610-11.
19. Ibid., p. 3611.
20. Fessenden to James S. Pike, Apr. 6, 1866, Roger B. Taney Mss., Library of Congress.
21. *Congressional Globe*, 39th Cong., 1st sess., Jan. 18, 1866, p. 310.

4

The Republican Alternatives in 1867: Internal Reconstruction (Alternative 3) or National Protection (Alternative 4)

Despite radical complaints, Republicans knew that they would have to restore the southern states to normal relations in the Union if they ratified the proposed Fourteenth Amendment.

There might be a struggle between radical and nonradical Republicans, but restoration was a certainty. As the moderate Republican weekly newspaper the New York *Nation* affirmed, "The South has now ... an opportunity to choose its own destiny."[1]

Yet it soon became apparent that white southerners were not going to leap at the quickest way out of the Reconstruction muddle, for while northerners regarded the proposed Fourteenth Amendment as an incredibly lenient settlement of the Civil War, most southern leaders were not going to acquiesce in several of its provisions if they could help it. The sections guaranteeing the national debt and repudiating the rebel debt, while distasteful, were acceptable. The provision reducing representation in Congress if southerners continued to exclude blacks from voting aroused more opposition, both because it plainly reduced southern power in the national government and because southerners still insisted that the national government had no right to involve itself in any way with state suffrage requirements.

Civil Rights and State Rights

But southern resistance centered on the other two substantive sections of the amendment. First, although southerners were willing—reluctantly—to eliminate racial discrimination in civil rights from their state laws if they had to, they did not want to write a civil rights section into the United States

Constitution. For generations southerners had resisted all efforts to give any control over race relations (in the form of slavery) to the national government. They had fashioned their arguments about state sovereignty, state rights, and limited national power with that end in mind—concepts that had been drilled into educated southerners with the fervor and authority of a religion. White southerners had fought a civil war because they were certain that the newly triumphant Republican party intended to violate those concepts. If it is not surprising that northerners demanded that the major issue of the war should be settled in their favor, we should not be shocked at southerners' reluctance to agree.

The constitutional amendment clearly recognized Congress's right to intrude into areas that used to be the business of the states alone. Republicans might say now that this expansion of power was more illusory than real, but who knew what kind of national action the amendment might sustain later? Southerners were a minority in the nation, and constitutional limitations on the power of the national government were their best defense against the power of the majority. As one southern newspaper expressed their fears, there might not be much we can do in defeat, but "one thing . . . we can do; we can avoid the fatal mistake of our fathers, so far as the constitutional power of defence has not wholly passed away. We can watch with jealousy and zeal the little that is left."[2]

Second, southern politicians bitterly assailed the provision of the Fourteenth Amendment disqualifying prewar southern leaders from office. Northerners could hardly understand the objection. Those southern leaders had sworn to uphold the Constitution of the United States and then rebelled against the government. Even the conservative New York *Evening Post*, which generally supported President Johnson through summer, 1866, marveled at southerners' recalcitrance. "The fact is that the men whom the amendment would exclude from office are guilty of what the laws declare a capital felony [treason], punishable with death," it pointed out. "The ineradicable and criminal selfishness of a small class . . . stands in the way of a just and speedy settlement of our difficulties."[3]

But the opposition of southern politicians ran deeper than the desire to retain their state offices. The amendment's disqualification section threatened to dismantle the southerners' political world as they had known and understood it. As in the rest of the United States in the mid-nineteenth century, political organization in the southern states was based on a system of mutual alliances between people with different spheres of political influence. Politicians knew who carried weight in different communities, and they sought alliances based on mutual advantages and cemented through the favors of the patronage system. Power was won and retained by the adeptness with which politicians fashioned such "friendships," and the experienced leader knew and understood the terrain of political influence; in 1865 southern politicians, large and small, knew who their political friends and enemies were, knew more or less what they had to do to win or retain power, and like their northern counterparts, identified this system as the practical workings of democracy.

The disqualification section of the proposed amendment promised totally to disrupt this political system. No one who held office before the war and then joined the rebellion—practically every substantial politician in the South—would be eligible to hold office after the amendment's ratification. Suddenly the entire political landscape would change; none of the old connections would work, none would even exist.

Despite all this, southerners might have ratified the Fourteenth Amendment in 1866 or January, 1867, if they had decided that they had no choice or if they had been absolutely certain that it was the last northern demand. But they knew that many radicals were insisting on more and that more conservative Republican leaders had been unable to pass the Reconstruction committee's bill promising restoration in exchange for ratification. But even more important was the conviction shared by President Johnson and his supporters in the North that the defeats of 1866 were not final.

When tentative movements developed in Alabama and Virginia to ratify the amendment, the president himself sent messages encouraging continued resistance. "What possible good can be obtained by reconsidering the constitutional amendment?" he asked. "I know of none in the present posture of affairs; and I do not believe the people of the whole country will sustain any set of individuals in attempts to change the whole character of our government by enabling acts [authorizing the organization of new state governments in the South] or otherwise. I believe, on the contrary, that they will eventually uphold all who have patriotism and courage to stand by the Constitution . . . . There should be no faltering . . . ."[4]

Even if the Republicans stuck with the Fourteenth Amendment rather than imposing black suffrage, Johnson's allies scented victory. After all, how long would northern voters put up with the present uncertainty? If southerners remained firm, northerners sooner or later would tire of waiting for ratification of the amendment and elect congressmen pledged to restoring the southern state governments immediately. So their northern friends offered southerners dangerous advice: "[L]et them do nothing . . . ." they urged. "Let them simply watch and wait. A masterly inactivity is the best policy they can adopt."[5] And southerners took it. In the entire South, only thirty-three state legislators voted to ratify the amendment. In three states it was rejected unanimously; it did best in Alabama, where it was defeated sixty-nine to eight in the state assembly and twenty-seven to two in the state senate.

Black Suffrage in the South

As they gathered in December, 1866 for the second session of the Thirty-ninth Congress, Republican leaders could barely believe the nearly unanimous southern decision to reject the amendment. A few, of whom Bingham and Fessenden were the most important, urged their colleagues to do nothing more, or at most to pass the Reconstruction bill rejected six months earlier—the one promising restoration for southern states ratifying the constitutional amendment. Others feared that Johnson and his allies were right in thinking that the voters would not put up with this kind of deadlock for long. Besides, they were angry. Nonradical Republicans had offered what they believed to be the most lenient possible settlement, in many cases surrendering their own convictions (especially on the justice of black suffrage) in the effort to restore harmony to the nation. "They would not cooperate [with us] in rebuilding what they destroyed," one of the moderates exploded. Now "we must remove the rubbish and rebuild from the bottom. Whether they are willing or not, we must compel obedience to the Union, and demand protection for its humblest citizen wherever the flag floats."[6]

Radicals rejoiced in the apparent conversion of their more cautious colleagues. With renewed vigor, they called for territorialization of the South, appointment of tried and true loyalists to power there, and black suffrage. Julian, Stevens, and Benjamin F. Butler (an influential Massachusetts politician just elected to the Fortieth Congress, which would meet in a few months) called for the disfranchisement of leading rebels and the confiscation of large estates and their redistribution to poor whites and blacks. Sumner and other radicals urged a national system of education for the South, or at least a nationally imposed requirement for free, equal education of all races.

Radicals had their first success when the House of Representatives passed a bill to reconstruct Louisiana. It provided for the organization of a provisional government, with only loyal men of both races participating as officers or voters. All laws the new government passed would be subject to congressional approval. When the provisional officers thought the people were ready to resume the normal functions of statehood, they could order the election of a convention to frame a new state constitution guaranteeing equal civil and political rights for all. If it were ratified by Louisiana's voters and approved by Congress, the state would resume normal relations with the Union. Meanwhile, the army would be responsible for protecting the people and enforcing the laws whenever the local authorities were unwilling or unable to do so.

At the same time that the House passed the Louisiana Reconstruction bill, the Reconstruction committee—speaking through Stevens—reported a bill dividing the South into military districts and giving commanders ultimate responsibility for all law enforcement. Its passage would impose direct national control over southerners while Congress hammered out Louisiana-like Reconstruction bills for the rest of the states.

Radicals believed that they had finally taken the first strong steps to settle the Reconstruction problem. If the Senate joined in passing the Louisiana Reconstruction bill and its precedent was followed in other southern states, then at least part of the radical program was assured. The bill dismantled Johnson's governments and placed southern loyalists in control, disfranchised rebels and enfranchised the freedmen, and put Louisianans under the indefinite control of Congress. It was the territorialization plan for which radicals had hoped. There would be time after it went into effect to consider confiscation and education laws, if the provisional government, dominated by black and white loyalists, did not decree those measures itself. But more conservative Republicans drew up short. Would the people of the North endorse such massive change in the South? Assuming that they were at last ready to sustain the imposition of black suffrage, would they wait patiently for restoration of the Union through years of territorialization? Would the businessmen of the North tolerate confiscation and redistribution of property?

Certain that the answer to all these question was no, the nonradical leaders—Bingham, Blaine, and others—developed an alternative program: they would agree to Stevens's bill from the Reconstruction committee putting southerners under temporary military control, but rather than follow it with a program of territorialization, confiscation, and education, they would amend the military government bill itself to include conditions for southern restoration. Southerners would only have to ratify the Fourteenth Amendment and frame new state constitutions enfranchising blacks and eliminating legal discrimination against them in order to be restored to the Union.

Of course, Johnson, northern Democrats, and most southern whites attacked the Negro suffrage provision bitterly, charging that it amounted to a total radical victory. But Republican congressmen understood that the "Blaine amendment," as it was called, was really designed to avert what radicals really wanted—long-term national control of the southern states until their political and economic institutions were fundamentally altered. The Blaine amendment specified that southerners could escape military rule simply by acquiescing in the nonradical Republican program of 1866 plus black suffrage (see Document 11-a).

The 1866 Reconstruction program was based on national protection for southern loyalists through the Fourteenth Amendment and the Civil Rights and Freedmen's Bureau acts; conservative and moderate Republicans hoped in early 1867 that by requiring black enfranchisement they had made such protection unnecessary. They adopted the radical view that the best way to protect black rights was to allow the freedmen to protect themselves through the ballot. Republicans were sure that southern politicians would not threaten the ex-slaves' rights if it meant alienating the entire black vote—a majority in some states and a large proportion of the total in all the others. So to a large extent the nonradical Republicans finally accepted the radicals' conclusion that Reconstruction could best be secured by internal change in the South rather than by a radical expansion of national power. As a Republican leader put it later, "Far from desiring centralization repugnant to the genius of this country, it is in the distinct interest of local self-government and legitimate State rights that we urge these propositions, and nothing can be more certain that this is the only way in which a dangerous centralization of power in the hands of our general government can be prevented." [7]

But the nonradical Republicans were accepting the radicals' conclusion without adopting their policy. By an internal reconstruction of southern institutions, radicals had meant more than the imposition of black suffrage alone and then the immediate restoration of the states to the Union. As Julian recalled, the radicals "warned the country, and foretold that no theories of Democracy could avail unless adequately supported by a healthy and intelligent public opinion. They saw that States must grow, and could not be suddenly constructed where the materials were wanting. . . ."[8] Years later, a disillusioned carpetbagger, Albion Tourgée, lambasted the new policy: Republicans gave the ballot to men without homes, money, education or security, and then told them to use it to protect themselves (see Documents 11-b and 11-c).

Fully understanding the essential conservatism of the Blaine amendment, radicals fought it bitterly in the House, finally defeating it there after a furious struggle. But in the Senate the nonradical forces triumphed. They buried the Louisiana Reconstruction bill and added the Blaine amendment to the Military Government bill. Recriminations on both sides were so bitter that it appeared for a time that no bill would pass at all, with the senators insisting on their version and radicals in the House opposing it as adamantly. But that meant stalemate—just what Johnson and his allies wanted—and both radical and conservative Republicans feared that they were playing into their opponents' hands. At last nonradicals agreed to modify the Blaine amendment enough to win the radicals' grudging consent to its passage (see Document 11-a). They added sections declaring the Johnson state governments to be provisional only, authorizing their removal by the military commanders if necessary, and they disfranchised the southern leadership (that is, the same people disqualified from holding office under the Fourteenth Amendment) in the election of delegates to new state constitutional conventions, in elections to ratify the new constitutions, and in any elections called to fill offices in the provisional governments. (In a supplementary Reconstruction act passed a month later, Congress instructed the military commanders to prepare new voting registries conforming to these provisions and outlined the procedures they would have to follow in administering elections.) The last minute amendments encouraged radicals to hope that the commanders would remove all the officials of the Johnson-supporting provisional governments and refill their positions through elections, virtually establishing the territorial-type governments they had wanted all along. Then these officials might have convinced the military authorities to delay the elections for the constitutional convention until they felt that true loyalty had been reestablished and citizens' rights were secure. But the radicals were to be disappointed. The military commanders interfered as little as possible with the old governments, and the old southern leaders remained substantially in power until the completion of the Reconstruction process.

Impeachment and the "End" of Reconstruction

After the Reconstruction bill passed (it was no longer called the Military Government bill because it now embodied a complete program of Reconstruction), events dashed any lingering hopes radicals held for a more thorough Reconstruction. If Republicans had felt that northern voters still supported them as firmly as they had in 1866, they might have followed radicals' advice and passed legislation confiscating rebel property, establishing equal education in the South, and giving blacks the vote throughout the United States. And they might have been less anxious to have southerners meet the conditions set forth in the Reconstruction act in a hurry.

But Andrew Johnson's continued opposition took its toll. Beaten in Congress and at the polls, he stubbornly encouraged southern resistance to the new Reconstruction laws. First, he tried to water down the law's application. Although the laws disfranchised former state and federal officials who had aided the rebellion, Johnson instructed the military commanders to permit anyone who swore that he was not covered by the disqualification to vote, whether they were lying or not. That forced Congress to pass still another Reconstruction act, requiring the commanders to make sure that southern voters were not lying about their past activities. Then Johnson sided with the officials of the provisional governments in disputes with the military commanders; when the commanders, exasperated beyond endurance, finally removed some of the most intransigent of the officers, Johnson, as commander in chief, ordered *their* removal in turn.

Angry radical Republicans responded by calling for Johnson's impeachment and removal from office. He was subverting the Constitution, they charged, by using his presidential powers to obstruct the laws instead of enforcing them as his oath of office required. But more conservative Republicans were afraid to take such an extreme step. Angry and frustrated themselves, they preferred to remedy Johnson's abuses by passing new legislation tying his hands—new Reconstruction acts, a tenure of office act requiring him to get Senate approval in order to remove civil officers of the government, and a law requiring all military orders to go through the War Department and the commanding general.

Johnson's aggressiveness and congressional Republicans' timidity demoralized the party. Northern state elections in the summer and fall of 1867 indicated a serious decline in Republican popularity. Intent on holding on to conservative votes, Republican leaders worked to moderate the radical elements of the party instead of pressing for further reform.

Nonetheless, when Johnson seemed openly to violate the new tenure law in 1868 by trying to remove the secretary of war without the Senate's consent, the Republicans in the House finally did impeach him. But the law was too vaguely worded, the proceedings seemed too partisan, the consequences of removal too frightening for a small minority of independent-minded Republican Senators. They joined Democrats to secure the president's acquittal by one vote.

As the impeachment drive sputtered, it became apparent that Johnson would be confirmed in his power to obstruct Reconstruction. Northern Republicans—even many radicals—advocated quick action under the Reconstruction laws instead of delay. They advised southern loyalists to be cautious in reframing their state constitutions in order to alienate no more northern voters. By July, 1868, all but three of the southern states had met the conditions set down by Congress, despite the president's obstructions. Under the watchful eye of the military, black and white southerners had elected constitutional conventions, uniformly under Republican control. The conventions had drafted new constitutions which satisfied the conditions embodied in the Reconstruction acts. Republicans hurriedly restored the states to normal relations in the Union, and in 1868 elected General Ulysses S. Grant to the presidency on a platform that assured voters that the issues of the war were settled and that the nation could look forward to a generation of peace. As if to cap their program, in 1869 they passed the Fifteenth Amendment to the Constitution, declaring that no state could deprive citizens of the ballot because of race, color, or previous condition of servitude (*Alternative 3:* see Document 12). The internal political change in the South was now written into the United States Constitution (and the amendment applied in the North as well, enfranchising a hundred thousand blacks there).

The battle was over, the North's triumph secured, the editors of the Chicago *Journal* exulted, "for all time. Reconstruction . . . can never again be brought into the arena of popular politics as a vital issue."[9]

Notes

1. New York *Nation,* Oct. 4, 1866.

2. Richmond *Enquirer,* Dec. 31, 1866.

3. New York *Evening Post,* Oct. 19, 1866.

4. Johnson to Lewis E. Parsons, Jan. 17, 1867, quoted in Edward McPherson, ed., *The Political History of the United States of America During . . . Reconstruction* (Washington, D.C., 1875), p. 353.

5. New York *Daily News,* Dec. 1, 1866.

6. *Congressional Globe,* 39th Cong., 2d sess., Feb. 8, 1867, p. 1104.

7. Carl Schurz, "The True Problem," *Atlantic Monthly,* vol. 19 (March, 1867), p. 377.

8. George W. Julian, *Political Recollections, 1840-1872* (Chicago, 1884), p. 305.

9. Chicago *Journal,* Nov. 10, 1868.

5

The Solution Fails: The Inadequacy of Black Suffrage (Alternative 3)

By its Reconstruction policy, Congress ultimately left it up to southern black and white loyalists to protect themselves through the ballot, without buttressing it with provisions for black economic or educational opportunity, and without providing any probationary period in which respect for black rights might grow. But by requiring new state constitutional conventions in each of the rebel states, Republicans had given southern loyalists themselves a chance to make more fundamental changes. Representatives of the newly organized state Republican parties dominated each of the conventions because their opponents had refused even to vote, and later, Republicans also won control of the new state governments framed by the constitutions. Here was a last chance to secure a firm foundation for the loyalists' political power, which relied so heavily on black men's ballots; a last chance to really effect the radical alternative.

Changes—and Resistance—in the South

But southern Republicans did not *want* to rely only on black votes for political power; many of the more conservative among them worked hard in 1867 and 1868 to avoid being labeled the black man's party. In some states, like Florida, Texas, and Virginia, resulting divisions among Republicans grew so great that they developed two hostile organizations. But even more radical southern Republicans hoped that they could somehow win substantial white support. So while they firmly defended the basic civil and political rights blacks won in the Reconstruction acts, they decided against enacting basic economic reforms for which northern radicals and blacks had hoped. In all the southern state conventions Republicans beat back Conservative* attempts

*Although most white southerners allied with the national Democratic party after 1865, many of them bridled at accepting the name. Many leading southern opponents of congressional Reconstruction had been staunch Whigs before the war; a large minority of them had even opposed secession in 1861 (although they fought for their states after the step was taken), and blamed Democratic agitators for the disasters which war brought. Rather than alienate anyone when they thought unity was essential, those who opposed the Republicans for many years called themselves *Conservatives*.

to require voters to meet education, literacy, or property qualifications, any of which would have disfranchised large numbers of former slaves. There was less unity on banning restrictions on office holding; but ultimately the right of black men to hold official positions was challenged only in Georgia. In the same way, Republicans uniformly insisted on the establishment of free, public school systems to educate the children of all races, and they established state-wide taxation to support them. But only in Louisiana and South Carolina did the constitutional conventions require that the schools be integrated (the requirement was never carried into effect, however), and many Republicans cooperated with Conservative efforts to require segregation, despite the eloquent pleas of a few farseeing black delegates that "the most natural method . . . [of removing race distinctions] would be to allow children, when five or six years of age, to mingle in school together. . . . Under such training prejudices must eventually die out."[1] Nonetheless, the establishment of free public school systems, in many states the first ever provided even for white children, was one of the most meaningful achievements of Reconstruction. Their creation, in the opinion even of most black leaders, far outweighed in importance the problem of their racial composition.

These important changes in the political and educational institutions of the South were as far as white southern Republican leaders felt they could go, and this marked the dilemma that southern Republicans faced. The fact was that the South was polarized along racial lines, and both northern and southern Republicans wanted to break down that polarization. If they went further and tried to improve black people's economic status or tried to meet their growing demands for political office and equal rights in streetcars, railroads, threaters, and other public facilities, then they surrendered any chance they had of winning at least some white support. But if they hesitated, they endangered their black support and risked being replaced as leaders by Republicans who would not be so reluctant to champion the interests of their constituents. To make matters worse, aside from the danger of losing black support, if the Republicans stopped short of forcing economic change, they would leave the black political power on which they depended without firm economic underpinnings.

In the end, the southern loyalists did not try to secure economic independence for the freedmen. Southern Republican delegates to the constitutional conventions did not want southern politics to be the medium for war between the races; they just wanted to win elections in the time-honored way—by fashioning appeals to various interest groups. In the economic provisions of their new constitutions and in their economic legislation of 1868-1869 they courted whites, not blacks. The closest any of the conventions came to distributing land was in North Carolina, where the delegates passed a resolution asking the legislature to provide freeholds for all citizens, through loans or other arrangements. In South Carolina, the convention passed a resolution calling for future legislation to create a state land commission to buy land and resell it to freedmen. The Texas convention passed a resolution granting lands out of the public domain to Texas Union army veterans, many of whom were black. None of these suggestions became law, but in a few states, especially Virginia, taxes were laid primarily on land in an effort to force the breakup of large estates and their sale to small landowners.

Rather than help ex-slaves gain property, many of the conventions enacted constitutional provisions and passed resolutions, put into effect by the military authorities, designed to help whites keep theirs. The Alabama, Georgia, Mississippi, and North Carolina conventions passed resolutions suspending the collection of debts, and radicals pressed the issue in Louisiana and Texas as well. Every convention increased the amount of property exempted for seizure in case of bankruptcy. Especially popular with the upcountry farmers, these "stay laws" and "homestead exemptions" were part of the Republican strategy to build an alliance between poorer whites and blacks in several states. Since these upcountry white farmers had often supported the most radical wing of the Jacksonian Democratic party before the war, several state conventions (those in Mississippi, Arkansas, Texas, and Virginia) also enacted Jacksonian prohibitions on state subsidies to private corporations, or made them difficult to get. Nonetheless, in practice nearly all the new Republican governments tried to win white support by trying to aid economic development through state action. They found ways to subsidize the construction of transportation facilities. Louisiana aided the development of a company to repair the war-damaged levees on the Mississippi River. Several states deposited state moneys and funded debts in ways designed to increase the availability of credit for investment in the economy.

The economic structure of the South did change significantly, but blacks were not the prime beneficiaries. Since the freedmen had no land of their own and since landowners did not have enough money to hire their labor outright, "sharecropping" replaced slave labor in many areas. The new system allowed the ex-slaves to work pieces of land individually, without the slavedriver's constant surveillance and intimidation, and it permitted them to establish their own homes separately from the old slave compounds, thus making possible a far greater sense of independence and self-worth. But this system left landowners with the power to eject unruly freedmen (especially active Republicans) from the land; generally left them in control of all marketing arrangements for crops, which often led to frauds against which the freedmen had no recourse; and slowly gave rise to "plantation stores," where destitute freedmen had to buy goods on credit in the winter and spring, and wound up owing nearly all the profit from their crops by summer and fall.

Wartime difficulties, the repudiation of Confederate bonds and money, the freeing of millions of dollars worth of slave property, and the higher rates of taxation that Reconstruction governments imposed to finance new educational and economic activities, forced the sale of many of the large plantations. In South Carolina, for example, by 1880 the number of plantations of over five-hundred acres would be cut by two thirds. The number of under-fifty acre landholdings rose from about 7,900 to about 36,000. In many cases this was the result of a deliberate Republican policy of high taxation of land to force its division and sale. But the benefits went to white small farmers, northern immigrants, and land speculators; rarely to ex-slaves. Southern states' promotion of commerce and industry at the expense of agriculture during Reconstruction, combined with general agricultural chaos caused by emancipation, caused economic and political leadership to pass from the hands of white plantation owners to white businessmen.

Battle Over Disfranchisement

Failing to secure a firm economic foundation for the political power of their black supporters, many southern white Republicans turned to the alternative of trying to shackle their Conservative opposition by disfranchising Confederate leaders and disqualifying them from holding political office. Missouri, West Virginia, Maryland, and Tennessee, all wracked by divided loyalties during the war, had disfranchised large numbers of rebels before 1865. In every state convention held in the South during 1867-1868, radical Republicans urged the disfranchisement of at least those rebel leaders who were prohibited from voting under the Reconstruction acts. It was the mildest conceivable punishment for rebellion and treason, they argued, and the only hope of neutralizing their enemies' superior talent and experience in political organization. But many northern Republicans, frightened by their losses in the fall 1867 elections, urged moderation on their southern allies. In most states, the voices for moderation were joined by the military commanders, whose opinions carried tremendous weight because southern loyalists' protection was in their hands. These cautious advisers argued that disfranchisement of former rebels would alienate the very white voters to whom Republicans were trying to appeal, that democracy could not operate where the most important members of the community were proscribed.

Disfranchisement provisions were incorporated into the new constitutions of Alabama, Arkansas, and Louisiana, but radical efforts to disfranchise the Confederate leadership were defeated in the Georgia, North Carolina, and Texas conventions after hard fights, and were hardly pressed in South Carolina at all. In Florida, disfranchisement was one of the most important issues in a bitter struggle that led a conservative Republican faction to oust a more radical one from the convention hall in a virtual coup d'état aided by the military commander.

The Virginia and Mississippi constitutional conventions also tried to disfranchise ex-Confederate leaders. But Mississippi voters refused to ratify their proposed constitution, and in Virginia, military commander John M. Schofield refused even to allow a vote. Conservatives and conservative southern Republicans urged Grant and Republican leaders in Washington to thwart efforts to disfranchise rebel leaders and to ease the enforcement of the Fourteenth Amendment's restrictions on ex-Confederates' rights to hold office. Hoping for an end to wartime bitterness and expecting that conciliatory gestures would strengthen Republicans' appeal to southern whites, Grant and the moderate Republicans agreed. They permitted Virginians and Mississippians to vote separately on the disfranchisement clauses of the proposed constitutions, and in both states the voters defeated the provisions. Grant instructed Virginia's military commander not to purge the new state legislature of representatives who were ineligible to office under the Fourteenth Amendment or Reconstruction acts, leaving the question to the legislature itself. In 1868, he had issued similar instructions to the military commander in Georgia. The Georgia legislature then admitted all elected representatives despite their questionable eligibility; the Virginia legislature did the same.

By 1869-1870 feeling was running so strongly against disfranchisement of ex-Confederates among most Republicans, including President Grant, that dissident Republican factions in Tennessee, Missouri, and West Virginia seized upon the issue in efforts to gain power. In each case, these self-named "liberal Republicans" appealed for Democratic support against the regular Republican organizations. In Virginia, too, Democrats combined with conservative Republicans, who had opposed disfranchisement there, defeating the regular organization in 1869. Alabama and Louisiana Republicans reenfranchised ex-Confederates in their states within a year after the adoption of the new constitutions which had disfranchised them. By 1870 disfranchisement of former rebels hardly existed and could not replace positive white support.

The Failure of Republican Strategy

Southern Republican economic policy did win some white adherents in a few states in the early years of Republican rule, but the loyalists were unable to enlarge or even retain it in most cases; they never won the firm, broad support they hoped for. (They had more luck in some of the border states, where counties which had stayed loyal during the war remain Republican strongholds even today.) There were several reasons for the failure. Naturally, large landowners resented the higher taxation brought by active state help to business, but most businessmen were also critical. They were especially repelled by the way Republican improvements increased state debts. Taxes alone could not meet the expenses. Instead, the Republican governments subsidized economic and educational development by issuing state bonds or guaranteeing bonds issued by private corporations. In the process, most of the Reconstruction governments contracted debts far in excess of those undertaken by prewar governments. Much of the debt existed only on paper, because the states would have to pay off bonds they guaranteed only if the companies that issued them went bankrupt. Even if that happened, the states would get the defaulting companies' capital assets. (In the case of railroads, the most important example, this meant that the states would get ownership of the tracks and equipment.) But the large debt frightened businessmen nonetheless. If anything went wrong, it was they and the plantation owners who would be assessed the taxes necessary to pay it off.

Moreover, the public at large was expected to benefit only "in the long run" from general economic growth stimulated by state aid. The most immediate benefits—railroad subsidies, contracts to construct public buildings, fees for floating state bonds—went to certain groups favored with good political connections. In North Carolina, a "ring" led by a North Carolina Conservative, George W. Swepson, and a northern immigrant Republican, Milton S. Littlefield, determined who received state aid, maintaining their influence with the Republican state legislature and governor through expert lobbying. Swepson's bank made trouble-free loans to legislators, never seemed to press for repayment, and cashed the legislators' pay slips at face value instead of at a discount, as other banks did. Swepson and Littlefield worked hardest to help the Chatham Railroad and the Williamston and Tarboro Railroad. At the same time, they managed to get control of the prize plum, the western division of the North Carolina Railroad, for themselves.

Swepson and Littlefield were also the chief beneficiaries of Florida's railroad subsidy legislation, purchasing two bankrupt Florida railroads with funds embezzled from their North Carolina railroad company and then persuading the Florida legislature to subsidize the extension of their lines to Mobile, Alabama. Instead of using the subsidy to lay track, Swepson and Littlefield made up the funds embezzled in North Carolina and lined their pockets and those of their co-conspirators. By 1871, the fraud was so apparent that the Florida legislature refused to aid any more railroads. In 1873 it repealed all subsidy laws; in 1875 Florida Republicans adopted a constitutional amendment barring state or local aid to railroads.

In South Carolina another ring, including some of the state's leading politicians, tried to win control of most of the state's railroad mileage. The ring used its influence to win favorable state administrative and legislative action, buying state-owned stock in railroads at favorable terms and embezzling state funds to pay for it. Opposed by businessmen with interests in other railroads, the South Carolina ring used its legislative clout to force a consolidation of its holdings with those of its former enemies, who then became allies.

Throughout the South, even where there was not such large-scale fraud, different groups of businessmen battled for control of southern state-aided economic institutions, especially railroads, and Republican legislation designed to win support often angered those who were not the direct beneficiaries. Friendly legislative action in Alabama won for the Republicans the support of V. K. Stevenson and his Nashville and Chatanooga Railroad, supported by Boston investors, but it alienated the management of its rival, the Louisville and Nashville. In Virginia, William Mahone organized the coalition of Democrats and conservative Republicans which elected his business associate, Gilbert C. Walker, governor in 1869, defeating Republican W. W. Wells and forcing the withdrawal of Conservative Robert E. Withers, both of whom favored his rivals' railroad interests. Tom Scott's Pennsylvania Railroad, Collis P. Huntington's Chesapeake and Ohio Railroad, and Henry Clews, one of Jay Cooke's many associates, sought to expand their holdings throughout the South, using their Republican connections wherever helpful, kindling the southern-patriotic resistance of such men as Mahone, Junius S. Morgan, and Captain E. N. L'Engle of Florida. (Once the Republicans lost power in the South, Scott and Huntington proved just as adept at winning Conservative confidence.)

Ultimately, Republican economic policy failed to attract permanent white adherents in the South; race proved to be more important to southerners than economics. Many southern leaders who flirted with republicanism learned that the vast majority of southern whites considered any southerner who cooperated with "carpetbaggers" (northern Republicans who migrated to the South) and freedmen to be a "scalawag," unfit for public life, business leadership, or social intercourse (see Document 13). Even those who benefitted directly from Republican legislation dared not affiliate with the party. In Virginia, Mahone regularly reassured Conservative associates of his fidelity, despite his ties to the conservative Republicans. In 1873 the Republicans nominated for governor a conservative Republican, Robert W. Hughes, who at first was friendlier to Mahone's interests than his Conservative rival. But Mahone and his business associates knew that if they supported the Republican they would lose their own influence in the state. *"Give Hughes every show you can,"* one of them wrote. "He is our friend even if we can't vote for him, under the circumstances."[2]

In North Carolina, Swepson, Kemp P. Battle, and Dr. William J. Hawkins all remained firmly Conservative despite the favors they received from the Republican government. Joseph E. Brown slowly backed away from his alliance with Georgia Republicans after 1869, despite Governor Bullock's aid to his railroad enterprises. Mrs. Rebecca Latimer Felton remembered with disgust that "scores of our ever-ready politicians hung around Governor . . . Bullock getting all they could out of him in jobs and positions, only to become ingrates and afterwards to abuse the man unmercifully . . . . They backed up this Republican governor in all his schemes for public plunder and then posed as Simon pure Democrats, immaculate and truly patriotic."[3]

Black Votes and the Southern Response: the Klans

The unwillingness of businessmen and white farmers to support state Republican parties in the South, despite economic legislation tailored to appeal to them, was a symptom of the fundamental Republican problem. No matter what else Republicans might do, they stood for black legal and political equality. In states with large black populations, such as Florida, Georgia, Louisiana, Mississippi, South Carolina, and Alabama, this meant black power—power to demand the kinds of civil rights, like equal access to schools, theaters, travel facilities, hotels, and restaurants, that inevitably would put blacks into socially equal contact with whites. Republicans—usually southern-born whites—who resisted black pressure for fear of alienating whites found themselves flung from power within the party by new leaders, often northern immigrants or blacks, who were willing to meet blacks' demands. By the 1870s blacks acquired more power in the southern Republican party than their northern allies had ever anticipated; most of its small number of white supporters deserted, unwilling to contemplate "social equality." Even many northern Republicans began to question the viability of state parties so solidly opposed by the wealthy, educated, and influential leaders of society.

But even more serious for white southerners was the effect of black equality upon the southern economy. The emancipation of the slaves and the guarantee of their civil rights worked a revolution in labor relations in southern agriculture. Under slavery, planters had been able to exploit black laborers by force. If blacks had been entitled to the same rights as whites, they could have demanded high wages because of the relative scarcity of labor compared to the great demand southern agriculture placed on it. Planters not only had paid no wages to their slaves, but they had forced them to work long hours and had forced women and children to work as well as men. Now that they were free, most black women left the fields, setting up as housewives or taking such domestic work as washing and sewing. Black families withdrew their children from the work force as well. Black men refused to put in the long hours they had been forced to work under slavery.

The consequence was a severe reduction in the effective southern labor force. With labor so scarce, black workers were able to demand the sort of compensation that slavery had been designed to avoid. Since planters needed workers to produce their crops and were denied the use of force under Republican governments, they wound up in intense competition among themselves to secure workers. Without the ready cash to pay high wages in any case, planters were forced to agree to black demands that they be allowed to work independently of close white supervision. The result was a variety of labor agreements that generally came to be called "share-cropping." By these agreements, planters provided land, seed, shacks, farm equipment, and sometimes animals, while workers planted, nurtured, and harvested the crop. The resulting crop was divided according to how much the planter provided and how scarce labor was.

White southerners bitterly resented the new system. They attributed the shortage of labor to black laziness, constantly lamenting the refusal of women to work in the fields and the unwillingness of black men to put in the long hours imposed under slavery. While planters considered themselves employers and therefore believed sharecroppers bound to obey their directives, the sharecroppers considered themselves partners, equally entitled to determine how to produce the crop. The result was friction. Planters tried to cajole sharecroppers into doing tasks that redounded more to the planter's benefit than the cropper's, such as repairing fences and shacks. The cropper preferred to put time into hunting, fishing, and cultivation of garden-plots, which augmented his food supply, and of course he wanted more time for leisure than he had been allowed under slavery. When workers refused to comply with their demands, planters again complained angrily about black laziness.

Planters made several efforts to regain control of labor. They tried to reach agreements among themselves regarding the wages they would pay or what sort of sharecropping agreements they would enter into. However, this could be considered "conspiracy in restraint of trade" and therefore was of questionable legality. Planters first tried it in 1865 and 1866, when the South was still under military occupation, and the military commanders and the Freedmen's Bureau had intervened to break the agreements up. The "black codes" passed by the Confederate-dominated governments organized under President Johnson's supervision had been designed to force the freedmen to remain agricultural laborers. The vagrancy provisions of the black codes put pressure on them to agree to labor contracts on planters' terms, by punishing them as vagrants if they were without work. But military commanders overturned these provisions too, and Congress eliminated the black codes altogether when it passed the Civil Rights bill. (See Documents 4 and 8b.)

When the southern states were restored to full rights in the Union, planters again tried to cooperate to limit concessions to workers. But there was no way to force one's neighbors to adhere to these understandings. Desperate for workers, planters continually broke ranks and wound up bidding for labor. To reduce the freedmen's leverage, planters tried to increase the labor supply by promoting immigration, even trying to bring in Chinese coolies. But all these efforts failed.

By the early 1870s it was clear that there was little southern planters could do to retain control of the labor supply as long as black workers' basic right to move freely from place to place and job to job was protected, and so long as local law enforcement officials resolved disputes between planters and sharecroppers fairly. Of all the demands black voters made of Republicans, protection of these rights were the ones they insisted on most rigorously, and they were the ones white southerners attacked most violently. Used to the old system, where all the tools of government power had sustained the rights of masters to exploit their workers, planters accused Republican sheriffs, district attorneys, and judges of promoting labor discord and insubordination by favoring black workers over white employers.

If this were not enough to alienate white southerners, Republican governments also raised taxes far above pre-war levels. There were several causes for the higher taxation. The Republican program of subsidizing economic development cost money. But more important were the new services the Republican governments provided--new state hospitals, asylums, and especially public schools. By freeing the slaves, Republicans had added to the number of citizens the government had to serve, while eliminating the slave property that had provided a large share of pre-war tax revenue. The result was not only an increase in taxes, but a shift in taxation from slaves to land at a time when planters faced rising labor costs and the necessity to borrow money to continue operations. Moreover, by shifting the tax burden to land, Republicans wound up taxing the property of the very white people whose support they had hoped to gain, the non-slaveholding small farmers of the southern upcountry.

Worst of all, since freedmen were poor, southern whites were called upon to pay nearly all the taxes, while black southerners received many of the benefits. Republican officials elected by mostly black votes distributed the revenue and received government salaries. Southern whites charged that blacks were using their power at the polls to confiscate the property of whites for the benefit of blacks, carpetbaggers, and scalawags. This was "class legislation"--a sort of socialism, where the poorer people used the power of government to seize the property of the wealthier.

Southern whites reacted bitterly to the new black power (see Document 14). As radicals had feared, the southern states had been restored to the Union before whites had learned to accept the legitimacy of black participation in politics. Even beyond its challenge to southern racism, black suffrage created too great a *practical* revolution in politics as southern politicians had known it to be accepted without the long period of tutelage radicals had wanted. None of the old political equations seemed to be valid any longer. One could win the ballots of ninetenths of the people who had voted before 1860, and still lose an election. One could gain the support of nearly all the men of influence in a community, the respected men of talent, education, and wealth who had always been the key to victory in years past, and still go down to defeat.

Blacks seemed impervious to the influence of traditional local opinion makers. They disappointed Conservatives who as late as 1872 still believed that blacks would take the political advice of landlords, employers, and former masters. Despite Conservative appeals, blacks voted as a unit for the Republicans. There was no way to deny the truth of what Republican campaigners so vigorously insisted—that the interests of black people in the South lay with the Republican party.

Frustrated and bitter at their inability to win black support through traditional campaign methods, Conservatives blamed the Republican-sponsored Union, or Loyal, Leagues for their failure. The leagues were social and political clubs to which many freedmen belonged. Like most fraternal organizations, they had secret rituals, symbols, and oaths, and white southerners, who had always feared the explosive potential of secret combinations of slaves, were certain that the leagues planned arson, assault, and other outrages. But worst of all, they were potent political forces. White southerners, refusing to admit the logic of overwhelming black support for Republicans, assailed the leagues as alien, illicit, undemocratic "machines" that voted the "ignorant" ex-slaves like "herds of senseless cattle."[4]

This was not democracy, southern whites believed; it was despotism. Northern immigrants and ambitious southern demagogues were winning control of southern state governments by the votes of an ignorant, gullible, inferior race. The new loads of state debt and the frauds perpetrated upon the Reconstruction governments, often by their own officers, proved the inability of black men to govern, southern whites insisted. Even moderate Conservatives believed that resistance to such governments was no crime, and the more restless among them soon put the conviction into action. The underlying fact was that the Republican state governments of the South did not enforce the laws and customs regulating race relations that nearly all white southerners believed right and necessary, and they did try to enforce others that most whites bitterly resented. Inevitably, southern ' whites tried to enforce the rules that Republicans rejected. They did it outside the law, sporadically and individually at first, and then in vigilante organizations, such as the most famous, the Ku Klux Klan.

Donning masks and grotesque costumes, swearing secret oaths, local Klans whipped and killed blacks whose conduct violated the unwritten southern laws of racial subordination (see Document 15). Blacks who challenged white authority, whether politically, socially, or economically, were the prime vigilante targets. In some areas white Republicans were also attacked. Spreading from Tennessee to Kentucky, the Carolinas, Georgia, Alabama, Mississippi, and Arkansas from 1868 to 1871, the loosely organized Klans enlisted the support of the social and political elite of the South; its activists were young whites from all classes. The Klans' ultimate aim, whether articulated or not, was to win by force what Conservatives could not seem to win through politics—control of the southern state governments.

Stunned by the fury and magnitude of the atttacks, southern Republicans hesitated. The ex-slaves, who were economically dependent on whites, poor, still uneducated, and without the yeoman farmer's self-respect that radical Republicans had hoped would come with land redistribution, did not respond with open violence. In most areas white Republicans were overwhelmingly outnumbered. Besides, in civilized nations it is the obligation of the government, not the individual citizen, to punish wrongdoing. But Klan members and sympathizers often sat on juries, preventing convictions. In other instances they intimidated jurors. In some areas of Klan activity local law enforcement officials were themselves members or sympathizers of the Klan. In other areas, the number of Klansmen made it impossible for sheriffs and constables to take meaningful actions. Desperate Republicans turned to their state governments.

After some hesitation, the governors of Tennessee, Arkansas, and North Carolina declared martial law and called out state militias. In Tennessee a new Republican governor withdrew the militia before it could do any good, in exchange for Conservative support against a more radical Republican at the next election. (He also agreed to allow disfranchised ex-rebels to vote without challenge.) But in Arkansas and North Carolina the militias quickly routed the Klans, arresting leaders and jailing them without trial.[5] But it was too late. North Carolina Conservatives won control of the state legislature in the 1870 elections, with the Republican vote falling dramatically in the counties where the Klan had been most active. The legislators impeached and convicted Governor Holden for exceeding his powers during the militia campaign and restored ex-Confederate control over the state. Only in Arkansas did use of the militia succeed in staving off Republican defeat.

The governors of Arkansas, Tennessee, and North Carolina could call on militias because there was still a strong minority of white Republicans in their states, and members of that minority were willing to serve. (Actually, the Arkansas militia was stiffened by volunteer Unionists from Missouri, and North Carolina's by volunteers from staunchly Republican east Tennessee.) But in South Carolina, Alabama, and Mississippi, Republican support among whites was minimal. The militia units which could be trusted against the Klan were all black, and to call them out meant to wage race war. The Republican governors of those states shrunk from that alternative. Governor Smith of Alabama, pressed by his party to do something, minimized the problem. So at first did Governor Scott of South Carolina.

In the face of the overwhelming economic and physical power of southern ex-Confederates, the black man's ballot was proving a fragile weapon. Unable to stem the inexorable flow of terror, or afraid to try, Republican state officials and citizens appealed to the national government for help. The alternative of an internal reconstruction of power in the southern states was failing. Only if the national government acted to preserve southern Republicans' right to a free ballot would the solution of 1867 have a chance to work. But that meant returning to the alternative of national protection that Republicans had rejected earlier because it promised too great an expansion of national power. Would the national government protect southern loyalists now, two years after Republicans had announced the end of war issues?

Notes

1. South Carolina Convention of 1868, *Proceedings of the Constitutional Convention of South Carolina* . . . (Charleston, 1868), p. 353-54.

2. Nelson M. Blake, *William Mahone of Virginia: Soldier and Political Insurgent* (Richmond: Garrett & Massey, 1935), p. 143.

3. Rebecca (Latimer) Felton, *My Memories of Georgia Politics* (Atlanta: Index Printing Co., 1911), p. 47.

4. *New York Herald*, quoted in Francis Butler Simkins and Robert Hilliard Woody, *South Carolina During Reconstruction* (Chapel Hill: University of North Carolina 1932), p. 80.

5. The essence of martial law is that it replaces ordinary law-creating and enforcing agencies with the will of the military commander. Generally, during martial law citizens' access to the privilege of the writ of habeas corpus is suspended, so that one may be jailed without trial until civil law is restored or until released by the commander.

6

National Protection (Alternative 4) or Conciliation (Alternative 5)

For national Republican leaders, the years 1869 to 1871 were a time of painful indecision. They were trapped again between their own commitment to maintaining the fruits of the Union victory as they saw them—loyalist control of the South and southern acceptance of American principles of legal and political equality for all men—and northerners' yearning for an end to the sectional trauma. And the problem was made worse by Republicans' promise, made too hastily during the presidential elections of 1868, that the war issues were finally settled.

Republican Indecision

Of course, there were political considerations to take into account. Strong southern Republican parties seemed essential to the party's continued political dominance. If Democrats established monolithic control in the South, it appeared impossible that Republicans could overcome for very long that disadvantage in presidential and congressional elections. But Republicans differed widely on how best to build a southern party.

Radical factions of the southern parties urged continued disqualification of Confederate leaders from holding office and continued disfranchisement where it existed, the appointment only of committed Republicans to national offices in the South, and protection for black voters and reliance upon them as the mainstay of southern Republicanism. More conservative southern Republicans insisted that the party had to expand its base by appealing to conservative whites, "the brains and the wealth of the South."[1] Like Democrats, they complained that corrupt demagogues had gained control of the party in the South "by appealing to the cupidity and passions" of the freedmen.

The views of southern Republican conservatives were echoed by many white southerners who had opposed secession in 1861 but who had finally fought for the Confederacy and cooperated with Republicans' opponents since the war. These "original Unionists," who generally had been Whigs before the war, insisted that they were eager to abandon their distasteful alliance with southern secessionist Democrats, if only Republicans would "do them justice, in a spirit of liberality, magnanimity." That meant "recognising ... and rewarding [with office] the men who braved the storm of secession in 1860, and 1861, from an unselfish love of the Union . . . . The exclusion of southern men of proven ability, purity of character, and national sentiment, from a participation in the offices of dignity and profit should cease . . . . "[2]

This advice strongly appealed to northern Republicans, and by the 1870s many of them were urging a "liberal" program of amnesty to all ex-rebels disqualified from office by the Fourteenth Amendment and an end to disfranchisement by the states. But these suggestions carried implications that made others pause. To follow them meant throwing overboard the more radical leadership of the southern Republican parties, conciliating conservative white southerners at the expense of radical blacks, and resisting black pressure for a larger share in running the southern governments and greater equality in education and public facilities. It meant sanctioning legislation designed to satisfy white employers more than black employees, white taxpayers more than black poor.

Making northern Republicans still more cautious was the fact that southern white conservatives never actually promised outright to change their political affiliations in exchange for control of the South. They merely affirmed that this was the only way that a strong Republican party *could* be built; they could not assure that the attempt would succeed. As one of them put it simply, "If the materials for the construction of a Union party do not exist in the party which opposed secesssion, [then] it does not exist in the South [at all]."[3]

While Republican leaders tried to decide in what direction southern Republicanism should develop, uncertainties in the North also affected them. The most important Republican congressmen had insisted that the congressional Reconstruction legislation after the war was a temporary aberration, justified because the nation was in a state of war and the southern states were being held in the "grasp of war." Most Republicans had vowed that the exercise of such exceptional congressional powers would cease when southerners met the terms set by the North for their restoration to normal relations with the Union. Southerners *had* met those terms; their states *had* been restored to their normal places in the Union. Would northern voters put up with a reopening of the question? Would they sustain still more legislation to help southern Republicans?

Adding to the reluctance to continue the Reconstruction battle was the increasing importance of other issues. Convinced that the war issues were settled, a growing number of the intellectual leaders in the Republican party—especially influential newspaper editors, academics, and New England brahmins—began to fight against what they believed to be an interrelated set of new evils. One was the wide acceptance of what these "reformers" saw as a false and dangerous financial doctrine—that the government should help business by inflating the currency. A second was the conversion of the high tariff on imported goods from a temporary measure to increase government revenue and to help prevent a few, infant industries from being destroyed by cheap foreign competition, to a permanent system designed to maintain high profits and wages in American industry.

In both cases, reformers charged that the powers of government were being used to help particular interests at the expense of society as a whole. In the case of deliberate inflation, debtors and "speculators" (a term of opprobrium which often just meant people trying to start new businesses) were helped, while creditors and established businessmen were hurt. In the case of the protective tariff, the beneficiaries were industrialists and the losers were the entire public, which had to pay artificially higher prices—practically a tax on the many to benefit the powerful few.

Despite their efforts, the reformers made little headway. Notwithstanding their education and intelligence, their ideas seemed to have little influence with Republican politicians. The more frustrated they became, the more they concluded that the problems lay in the nature of American political institutions. Democracy allowed, even required, politicians to pander to the popular passions. Politicians were interested only in office and they would do whatever was necessary to attain it. The public good counted very little, if it counted at all. American democratic institutions were demoralized. The signs were everywhere—the wholesale bribery of state legislatures and judges by railroad interests; the notorious venality in the city governments; the corruption in the civil service; the influence of demagogues like Ben Butler of Massachusetts and machine politicians like Pennsylvania's Simon Cameron, Indiana Senator Oliver P. Morton, and Zachariah Chandler of Michigan; the popularity of the inept President Grant. The power of special interests in tariff and fiscal matters were merely elements in the pervasive decay.

Certain of the accuracy of their assessment, the reformers added improvement of the national civil service to their other causes. Government appointments should be based on merit rather than political connections, they insisted, and appointees must retain their positions for life unless they misbehaved. National civil service reform would strike at the patronage system, the heart of the machine politicians' power; it would break the back of the unprincipled state and local party leaders who sought power for power's sake alone and who often winked at corruption; and it would open the way for the emergence of new leaders dedicated to the incorporation of correct principles into government.

The reformers at first hoped that President Grant would support them. If so, their battle would be largely won, because the patronage system depended upon the cooperation of the president, who appointed all federal officers. If he ignored the requests of state and local party leaders in staffing the civil service, the reformers' job was done, and the bosses' political machines would soon collapse. But Grant, who had prided himself on his political independence before he became president, decided that he could win support for his policies—especially his foreign policy—most easily through the traditional political system. Like presidents before him, he rewarded politicians who supported by him by giving them access to government patronage, and he punished his opponents by withholding it. Traditional party leaders quickly rallied to his side in order to maintain their positions; the disillusioned reformers, doubly angry because they felt betrayed, began to focus their efforts on preventing his renomination and replacing him with a Republican candidate who would champion their cause.

As they struggled against Grant and the regular party organizations of their states, these Republican reformers also grew progressively more hostile to further northern agitation of Reconstruction issues. Disturbed by the willingness of poor and uneducated northern masses to support demagogues like Butler, machine politicians like Chandler, and crooks like Boss Tweed of New York, they began to reconsider their wisdom in imposing black suffrage on the South. When southerners complained of the corruption and wastefulness of their Republican black and carpetbag governments, the reformers credulously believed them. They became more and more convinced that northern Republican support for their southern allies was motivated by the desire to retain power rather than by principle. They charged bitterly that Republican leaders were using the Reconstruction issue in the 1870s to deflect the public from general reform. Identifying with southern Republican "liberals" who opposed continued disfranchisement of whites and reliance on blacks for political power in their states, the reformers also came to be called "liberal Republicans." By 1871, "liberal Republicanism" stood for an end to radical policies in the South, an end to the protective tariff, opposition to inflationary financial policies, and reform of the civil service.

Meeting and corresponding with one another regularly after 1870, the dissidents challenged orthodox Republican leaders on a wide range of issues. They made their views known through their control of important Republican newspapers and journals—the *North American Review*, the *Nation*, the *Independent*, the St. Louis *Democrat*, the Springfield (Mass.) *Republican*, and the most influential Republican paper in the East, the *New York Tribune*, and in the West, the *Chicago Tribune*. Although few congressional Republicans openly challenged their leaders, many of them sympathized with the liberal position on varying issues. Within the state parties, Republican factions began to adopt the liberals' ideas as weapons against more traditionalist party rivals. By mid-1870 one Republican senator lamented, "The Republicans are of one party only in name—and each leader is the representative of a faction in deadly hostility to some other faction inside the organization."[4]

Ex-Confederates Begin to Regain Power

With the party in such disarray, it seemed impossible for Republicans to establish a strong policy in response to the disintegrating position of their southern allies. By 1870 ex-Confederates had regained control of Georgia, Tennessee, Virginia, and North Carolina, as well as the loyal border states of West Virginia and Missouri, through cooperation with dissatisfied Republicans, and through fraud and violence.

In Virginia, where the voters were to ratify or reject their new constitution in 1869 (it was one of the three states which had not met the conditions of the Reconstruction act in 1868), Conservatives coalesced with conservative Republicans. At their request, President Grant allowed Virginians to vote separately on whether or not they wanted disfranchisement and officeholding restrictions in the new constitution. Claiming Grant's support, the coalition won the election, defeating the two provisions, ratifying the rest of the constitution, electing the governor, and winning control of the state legislature. When Republicans challenged the eligibility of ex-rebels to take seats in the legislature until Congress recognized the new state government, Grant ordered the military commander, General E. R. S. Canby, not to interfere, and the former Confederates got their seats. In Missouri, Democrats followed a similar strategy in 1870, allying with that state's liberal Republicans, who favored repeal of anti-Confederate political restrictions. In both states the coalitions' success paved the way for complete Democratic and Conservative victories a few years later and Democratic domination through the nineteenth century.

In other states, ex-Confederates regained power through more unsavory, often illegal methods. In Tennessee, as in other border states with divided loyalties, rebels had been disfranchised during the war, and that restriction remained when Congress restored the state to normal relations with the Union in 1866. Ex-Confederates' resentment fueled a powerful Ku Klux Klan movement, which had seriously weakened the Republicans by 1868. After long hesitation, in 1869 Governor William G. Brownlow called out the state militia to protect Republicans. But when he resigned to enter the United States Senate, his successor, DeWitt C. Senter, recalled the militia and advocated repeal of the disfranchisement laws. Senter's decision divided the party; more radical Republicans nominated William B. Stokes for governor, while liberal Republicans and Conservatives supported Senter. To assure victory, Senter ordered voting registrars to ignore the disfranchisement laws and allow former rebels to vote. The influx of new voters carried Senter and his allies to victory. Although Senter was nominally a Republican, the election had driven him into the arms of the Conservatives, and the success was really theirs; the Republican party went into eclipse, winning only one state election between 1870 and 1910.

In West Virginia, liberals won control of the Republican party by 1870. Since West Virginia had remained loyal to the Union, it had not been subject to the Reconstruction acts, and blacks were not yet allowed to vote. But here too rebels had been disfranchised. Now, with liberals taking the lead, Republicans endorsed universal suffrage for both ex-rebels and ex-slaves. But Democrats, endorsing an end to white disfranchisement, continued to oppose political privileges for blacks. In the bitter election of 1870, a Democratic federal judge ordered the arrests of voting registrars who enforced the state's disfranchisement laws. With large numbers of ex-Confederates voting, the Democrats won the election and established a political hegemony that lasted until the 1890s.

North Carolina fell to the Democrats largely as the result of Ku Klux Klan violence. Responding reluctantly to desperate pleas for protection from Republicans in central and north-central counties, Governor Holden called out the state militia during the 1870 state elections. Nevertheless, the Republican vote fell by 12,000 compared to its 1868 total. The Conservative vote increased by only 3,000. So at least 9,000 Republican voters of 1868, more than enough to overcome the Conservatives' victory margin of 4,200, stayed home, either out of fear or disapproval of their party's course. The new Conservative legislature threw out Republican representatives from districts where Holden had stationed the militia and proceeded to impeach and remove Holden himself. Once again the Republican defeat proved final. Grant carried the state in 1872, but demoralized Republicans could not win a state election until 1894, and then only by allying with the new Populist party.

By far the most complex case, and the only one in which congressional Republicans sought to stem the tide, was Georgia. There conservative Republicans allied with Conservatives as early as 1868, admitting to the state legislature members who were ineligible under the Fourteenth Amendment and ejecting black representatives because, they insisted, the state constitution only gave them the right to vote, not to hold office. That gave complete control of the legislature to Conservatives, but despite the urging of Governor Bullock and other Republicans, Grant and Congress did nothing until December, 1869, over a year later. Then, with reports of Ku Klux Klan outrages multiplying, Congress at Grant's suggestion put the state back under military control, instructing General Alfred H. Terry to restore the black legislators and purge ex-Confederates who could not take the Test Oath required of state officials by the Reconstruction acts.

The process was not complete until January, 1870. New state elections were only a few months away, and the events of the prior eighteen months had badly demoralized the Republican party. Desperately, Bullock lobbied congressional Republicans to add to any bill restoring Georgia's rights in the Union a provision postponing new elections for two years. Although radicals like Butler, Chandler, and Sumner tried to include such a provision in the Georgia Restoration bill, Bingham, Trumbull, and other nonradical Republicans prevented it, and Georgia Conservatives easily won the fall elections. Rather than face the inevitable impeachment proceedings, Bullock resigned, and by 1871 Georgia too was firmly in the grip of ex-Confederates, and has remained Democratic to this day.

Border state and Upper South Republicans pleaded for congressional action. Virginia radicals urged their congressional allies not to restore their state to the Union while Conservatives retained control, or at least to require state legislators to take the oath required by the Reconstruction acts. "Whether the Republican Party in this state, and the whole south shall survive or sink is the question ... " they insisted.[5] But conservative Virginia Republicans advised caution. "Many intelligent Republicans fear that [imposition of the Test Oath] ... would give us a Legislature which would do the permanent interest of the Republican party in the State irreparable harm," warned one loyal but cautious Virginia leader.[6] Many conservative southern Republicans similarly countered the radicals' arguments, insisting to Republican leaders that the radicals represented the worst elements of southern society. The Republican party must not alienate forever the respectable southern whites who opposed federal interference, they cautioned.

With President Grant urging Virginia's restoration and admitting his reluctance to interfere anywhere in the South, with northern public opinion divided between the desire for peace and the desire to maintain loyalist supremacy in the South, and with liberals in their own party opposing further Reconstruction measures ("The question underlying all this controversy is a very simple one," wrote the *Chicago Tribune*. "Is the war ended? Will it ever end?"), the congressional Republican leadership sidetracked radical efforts to succor their southern friends.[7] Virginia was restored to the Union; a bill to place Tennessee back under military control, sponsored by Butler, was stalled by House Speaker Blaine and finally buried.

By mid-1870 southern Republicans numbly realized that Congress would not reverse their local defeats. "Union and Loyal citizens will be left out in the cold, or what is worse, be at the mercy and beck and call of a set of Rebels whoes hands are yet red with the Blood of Loyal men," lamented a Tennessee Republican. "Great God is there no hope, and are men who stood by the Government now at this late day to be sugugated and controled by the Enimes of the Government?"[8] Butler, furious but helpless in the face of the opposition of other Republican leaders, received this short, anguished note from a Virginia radical:

> Into the hands of American traitors we must go.
> Wish I could make Congress see things as they are.
> Terrable thought that we must be handed over to Rebels
> In Gods name save us if you can.[9]

The Republican Response: The Force Act

Public opinion and dissent among their own leaders made it impossible for congressional Republicans to resume direct control over southern states as they had over Georgia. Instead, after long hesitation, the Republicans returned to the alternative that they had rejected when they passed the Reconstruction acts—direct national protection of their southern allies. When the Fifteenth Amendment was ratified early in 1870, Republicans passed a law to enforce it. The Enforcement Act of May 31, 1870, made it a federal crime to bribe or intimidate voters and, in a section aimed directly at the Klans, made criminal all conspiracies to deprive citizens of any rights or privileges. But the law came too late to save Virginia, Tennessee, Georgia, West Virginia, Missouri, and North Carolina. In fact, because only in North Carolina could the Republican debacle be blamed solely on violence, the law probably could not have helped anyway. Although the Klans rode in

Tennessee and Georgia, and there was plenty of non-Klan violence in the other states, the Conservatives regained power there through either legitimate alliances with dissident Republicans or fraudulent violations of state disfranchisement and officeholding qualification laws, which the new Enforcement Act did not cover.

Moreover, the Enforcement Act alone proved ineffectual against the Klans. Although it authorized federal marshals and attorneys to enforce the law in federal courts, which were more reliable than state courts, the peace officers, witnesses, judges, and juries were still liable to Klan intimidation and harassment. Often Klansmen had the support of entire white communities. Grand juries regularly refused to indict suspects even in the face of compelling evidence. As a result, in 1870 the law was enforced with vigor only in Tennessee, where marshals arrested 190 men. With that exception and some very limited activity in Kentucky and North Carolina, there were no arrests, and nightriding and terror increased in Alabama, Mississippi, Georgia, and South Carolina, while in North Carolina it continued unabated until the Conservative election victory that fall.

By December, 1870, Republicans faced the stark fact that violence threatened to sweep away the reconstructed, Republican governments of the entire South. Appeals from southern Republicans continued to flood Congress and the Justice Department. Desperate radicals, led by Butler, tried to force consideration of a stringent Reconstruction bill, but they were thwarted by the expert parliamentary maneuvering of the more conservative Republican leaders—Garfield, Blaine, Dawes, Bingham, and John A. Peters. Butler and Blaine assailed one another furiously on the floor of the House, as the spirits of disillusioned southern Republicans sank in the wake of Congress's apparent impotence. "Alas I fear they have not spirit and honest manhood enough to stand up like men against the assassins of the South," one southern loyalist wrote despondently. "What an example to the world we are. A nation that cannot protect its own citizens."[10] Others reacted with a sudden, exasperated burst of disloyalty. "Any Government that does not protect its subjects *does not* deserve the name and deserves to come to an end as it will."[11]

By now rank and file congressional Republicans were at the brink of open revolt against their conservative leaders. Southern Republican governors and state legislators were preparing to call upon the president formally for troops to put down "domestic insurrection." Unwilling to answer the state governments' calls for military aid unless he could share the responsibility with Congress, on March 23, 1871, Grant personally came to the Capitol to encourage congressional action. At last the conservative Republican leadership decided that it could hold out no longer, and within a few days a special committee reported what came to be known as the Ku Klux Klan, or Force, Act.

But Republicans' original—and in many cases continuing—constitutional conservatism came back to haunt them. The committee's bill declared that conspiracies to commit ordinary crimes, like murder and assault, which had always been in the states' jurisdiction, violated the constitutional rights of United States citizens, and could be punished by the national government. When widespread domestic violence threatened those rights, failure of the states to protect their citizens amounted to denial of the "equal protection of the laws" guaranteed by the first section of the Fourteenth Amendment, and the president could use military force, declare martial law, and suspend the privilege of habeas corpus in order to provide protection.

Already upset because they were being forced to legislate in states no longer in "the grasp of war," Republican constitutional conservatives joined Democrats to challenge the breadth of the bill. Democrats and the most conservative Republicans insisted that the civil rights section of the Fourteenth Amendment merely banned discriminations in state laws, that it never gave Congress power to punish the acts of individuals. Other doubtful Republicans conceded that Congress could punish violations of civil rights by individuals, but only in a limited way. It could not enact a law against murder, with one punishment; another against assault, with a lesser punishment; another against arson, etc. To do that would be to enact a national criminal code replacing those of the states. Congress could punish only one basic crime under the first section of the Fourteenth Amendment— violation or conspiracy to violate civil rights, no matter whether done by murder, beating, or anything else. Moreover, national authorities could punish that crime only if the states failed through by inaction to provide equal protection of the laws. "The great war for the Union has vindicated the centripetal power of the nation, and has exploded, forever I trust, the disorganizing theory of State sovereignty, . . . " Garfield said as he opposed the original version of the bill. "But we should never forget that there is danger in the opposite direction. The destruction or serious crippling of the principle of local Government would be as fatal to liberty as secession would have been fatal to the Union."[12]

When Bingham, who had proposed the civil rights section of the Fourteenth Amendment, insisted that he had always intended to give Congress the power to enforce it against individuals, Garfield reminded him of how concerned Republicans had been to protect states' rights when they passed the amendment, back in 1866. "My colleague can make but not unmake history," he said gently.[13]

Faced with strong Republican opposition, the bill's sponsors modified it to meet some objections (see Document 16). The list of ordinary crimes was eliminated; a provision allowing the president to use the state militias against the Klans was deleted; a section added by the Senate holding entire counties liable for damages and injuries inflicted by armed guerillas was dropped. The operation of the martial law and habeas corpus sections were limited to the end of the next session of Congress. Even these modifications did not satisfy the most cautious Republicans. The measure was still a shockingly bold use of national power. Many of those who were identifying openly with the liberal wing of the party clearly announced their opposition and abstained on the final vote.

The passage of the Force Act, hesitating as it was, did not mark a new radicalism in Washington. It was the bare minimum Republicans could do, after long delay, to prevent the total collapse of the reconstructed governments. With black voting power in the South inadequate to maintain loyalist control or protect ex-slaves' rights, Republican leaders vacillated between making a firm display of national power and conciliating southern whites. At the same time that they wielded the stick of the Force Act, they offered the carrot of the Amnesty Act, which removed the Fourteenth Amendment's officeholding disabilities from all but a few hundred of the most eminent former Confederates.

The policy seemed to work. Although Grant tried to avoid sending troops to the South, he was finally forced to intervene in South Carolina. Southern Conservatives and northern Democrats assailed him violently. Liberal Republicans lamented further "centralization" and warned darkly that the nation was peering into the abyss of military dictatorship, but the army made short work of the terrorists. Inspired by the success, law enforcement officers in other states began to arrest and prosecute Klansmen with more vigor, even without army help. Although these offensives were scattered, the bare threat of greater vigilance on the part of federal officials seemed to have an effect. In Georgia and North Carolina, where Conservatives had already regained power, or in areas where Klan activity now threatened to bring down the full force of the law, white leaders turned against the Klan. It had served its purpose and now did more damage than good. By 1872 the Ku Klux Klan virtually ceased to exist.

Republicans also reaped political rewards. Congress took evidence on Ku Klux outrages to justify its legislation in the face of Democratic and liberal Republican attacks. The information that the investigators made public before the 1872 presidential elections was even more shocking than Republicans had expected and restored many wavering Republicans firmly to the party. When liberal Republicans and Democrats united to oppose Grant's reelection in 1872, emphasizing civil service reform and conciliation of the South more than tariff and financial reform, even more Republicans returned to the fold. Grant's victory at the polls was overwhelming. He carried the entire North and, significantly, all of the southern and border states but Kentucky, Maryland, Missouri, Georgia, Tennessee, and Texas.

But although Republicans were momentarily satisfied, they would quickly learn that they had merely postponed the inevitable decision whether to protect the fruits of victory by national action, or abandon the attempt. With the Klans dissolved, the state Conservative parties (which now called themselves "Democrats" more and more often) took over the Klans' role. In a series of virtual coups d'état they overthrew the remaining Republican governments and ultimately forced the nation to face the possibility of a second civil war.

Notes

1. J. J. Giers to David P. Lewis, Nov. 26, 1870, Papers of the Committee on Reconstruction, House of Representatives, 40th Cong., Record Group 233, National Archives, Washington, D.C.

2. Ibid.

3. Ibid.

4. Senator Daniel D. Pratt, quoted in the Cincinnati *Commercial,* June 9, 1870.

5. Thomas M. Brown to Benjamin F. Butler, Dec. 10, 1869, Files of the Select Committee on Reconstruction, House of Representatives, 41st Cong., Record Group 233, National Archives.

6. Richard W. Hughes to Butler, Jan. 10, 1870, ibid.

7. *Chicago Tribune,* Jan. 15, 1870.

8. H. P. Cleveland to Representative William B. Stokes, April 14, 1870, Stokes Mss., Tennessee State Archives, Nashville, Tennessee. Spelling as in original.

9. Burnham Wardwell to Butler, Jan. 17, 1870, Files of the Select Committee on Reconstruction, House of Representatives, 41st Cong., Record Group 233, National Archives. Spelling as in original.

10. Oliver Potter to Butler, Mar. 20, 1871, Butler Mss., Library of Congress, Washington, D.C.

11. Harlow Roys to Butler, Mar. 17, 1871, Butler Mss.

12. *Congressional Globe,* 42d Cong., 1st sess., April 4, 1871, appendix, p. 149.

13. Ibid., April 4, 1871, p. 151.

7

The Bitter Fruit of Victory: The Failure of National Protection (Alternative 4) and the Return to Conciliation (Alternative 5)

The Ku Klux Klan (Force) Act was a one-time affair, made necessary by the Klan's guerilla war against Republicans in the South. Faced with the choice of intimidating white southerners or conciliating them, Republicans still preferred the latter alternative. Even before the 1872 elections, they refused to extend the time period in which the president could suspend the habeas corpus privilege or proclaim martial law under the Ku Klux Act. At the same time, they rejected efforts of Sumner, Butler, and other radicals to link the passage of the Amnesty Act to acceptance of a new comprehensive Civil Rights bill that would guarantee the access of all Americans to facilities and businesses open to the white public at large. Despite Sumner's plea, "You must be just to the colored race before you are generous to former rebels," Congress passed the Amnesty Act while it let the Civil Rights bill die.[1] In the end, only one Republican senator joined Sumner in formally recording his opposition. (In the House of Representatives the Amnesty Act passed without a roll call vote so that congressmen would not have to go on the record.)

Grant's Hopes for Conciliation

Republicans' overwhelming victory over the liberal Republican-Democratic opposition in the 1872 presidential and congressional elections was won in large part by emphasizing the record of Ku Klux Klan outrages in the South to restive Republican voters critical of their party and president on other issues. Thereafter, Republicans worked hard to avoid Reconstruction action. One reason for the hands-off attitude was that President Grant had always hoped for a good relationship with the South. He had won election in 1868 by urging, "Let us have peace," and he had not intervened in the South until Klan violence had forced his hand. In the winter of 1872-73, he informed Congress that while he would continue to enforce the laws protecting citizens' rights, "It is ... regretted by no one more than myself, that a necessity has ever existed to execute the 'enforcement act.' No one can more desire than I that the necessity of applying it may never again be demanded."[2]

Southern Democrat-Conservatives and conservative Republicans began to press Grant to pardon or drop charges against former Ku Kluxers; the president was receptive. At first he refused to consider mass pardons, but after the 1872 elections his attorney general instructed district attorneys to press "pending prosecutions ... only as far as may appear to be necessary to preserve the public peace and prevent future violation of the law."[3] In 1872 the government dropped 203 of the 225 cases pending in Tennessee. By January, 1873, many southern Republicans were complaining. "If the mercy of the President were appreciated by these secessionist Democrats, we would have nothing to say against the prisoners being pardoned by wholesale," one of them wrote, "but when the Ku Klux regard it as an indication of weakness on the part of the Government, as they do now, we consider that the letting loose of the assassins once more is a wrong done to the loyal men of the South."[4] Despite such warnings and the protests of local law enforcement officials ("My labor is all gone for naught," lamented one[5]), in 1873 United States attorneys dropped about half the cases that had been pending at the beginning of the year. In 1874 they dropped nearly all the rest. Grant made his distaste for continued national intervention in the South so clear that by early 1874 many southerners believed he intended to break with the Republican party, and for a short time they talked about fashioning an alliance with northern conservative Republicans and moderate Democrats to support his candidacy for a third term.

Grant's desire to restore normal national harmony inclined Republican leaders to resist radical pressure, but political disasters in 1873 convinced many of them that they had no choice. Not until one hundred years later, when the Watergate scandals brought about a similar political reversal, did a successful political party lose ground so fast. Just after the Republican landslide of 1872, Garfield wrote from Washington that there was literally "no opposition" to Republicans in Congress. The Democrats "are stunned, perhaps killed by their late defeat and there seems no limit to the power of the dominant party."[6] But when congressmen voted themselves a retroactive increase in pay (the so-called Salary Grab) and the extent of the Credit Mobilier bribery scandal became known, implicating former Vice-President Schuyler Colfax, House Speaker Blaine, Garfield, and others, Republican support collapsed.

Heading for a probable catastrophe in the congressional elections of 1874, most Republicans hoped that they would not be forced to consider further decisive action in the South. Tales of fraud and corruption in the southern Republican governments, exaggerated by the Democratic and liberal Republican press, seemed to compound the scandals in Washington. Republicans were drowning in a tidal wave of cynicism. The people—and even many of the Republican leaders themselves—seemed to believe every accusation. Even northern Republicans called their southern white allies "carpetbaggers" and "scalawags." Protests that the name-calling was Democratic propaganda were ignored. At the time that "reformers" were most critical of Republican corruption, the southern governments came to symbolize that corruption. There seemed to be no way to maintain Republican ascendancy in the North, much less the nation, unless the reformers could be brought back into the fold.

On the other hand, Republicans watched with dismay as one by one the remaining Republican governments of the South tottered and fell. If something were not done, every southern and border state would soon be in the control of ex-rebels. Republicans would be faced with a solidly Democratic South, presenting their political opponents with a firm base of one third of the seats in Congress and about half the electoral votes needed to elect a president. What was worse, that solid Democratic base would be established despite the fact that almost half the voters in the South were Republicans (unfortunately, *black* Republicans).

Republicans faced damning alternatives: to rescue southern Republicans and alienate restive northern Republicans who thought "reform" more important than sustaining what they believed were corrupt carpetbag governments; or to conciliate the reformers and conservative Republicans and lose the rest of the South.

Paralyzed, Republicans again seemed unable to respond to the southern Republican collapse. In some states Democrat-Conservatives literally attempted revolutions; in others they regained power through apparently legitimate political action. But even where they succeeded at the polls, the normality was superficial. Republicans had restored the southern states before they had established the mutual respect and sense of fairness between factions and races necessary for democracy to work. Southern Republicans and Conservatives were not waging ordinary political contests over who would govern for the next few years; they were engaged in a life and death struggle. One side aimed to preserve and extend the changes wrought by a great civil war, the other to overturn them. The battle, though channeled through the ballot box, was not fought with decorum. Each side felt justified in cheating and intimidating the other if necessary or even merely helpful. In the several states where Republicans would probably win fair elections (South Carolina, Louisiana, Florida, and perhaps Alabama), Democrats perpetrated the frauds and the violence. Where the combatants were more evenly matched, as in Texas and Arkansas, Republicans often did the cheating while Democrats intimidated the voters. Republicans occasionally used force too, especially where black Republicans kept wavering blacks in line. This was not democratic politics. It is a mark of the failure of the Republican Reconstruction policy of 1867-68 that Republicans ever thought there could be.

The Republican Collapse in the South

The first state to fall after the 1872 elections, and the state where the Republican defeat was cleanest, was Texas. Factional rivalries had divided the party, as they did in every southern state, with many white Republicans alienated from Edmund J. Davis, the Republican governor. In 1872 Democrats and Liberal Republicans had won the congressional elections and gained control of the state legislature. They probably would have won the 1873 gubernatorial elections honestly, but they decided to make sure. In the words of the southern, pro-Democrat historian who has written the most thorough account of Texas Reconstruction, "The whites were determined that E. J. Davis would never again rule over Texas, that radical-carpetbag-negro domination was to be ended. It was in a sense a revolution. There is no shadow of a doubt of fraud and intimidation at this election. 'Davis negroes' were in many communities ordered to keep away from the polling places, while white men under age were voted." The Democrats won by a two to one margin. In the same historian's words, "The total [vote] was surprisingly large."[7] (The possibility that Democrats had stuffed the ballot boxes did not seem to occur to him.)

In January, 1874, Davis succeeded in having the Texas courts set the election aside on a technicality, but the Democrats were not to be thwarted. Rather than appeal the decision, they seized the state capitol, and the United States marshal telegraphed Washington that "a conflict seems inevitable."[8] Desperately, Davis telegraphed President Grant, asking him to fulfill the national government's constitutional obligation to protect states from "domestic violence," but the attorney general answered that "your right to the office of Governor at this time is at least so doubtful that he [Grant] does not feel warranted in furnishing United States troops in holding further possession of it, and he therefore declines to comply with your request." Bitterly, Davis protested that the president had "made a serious mistake," but he had no choice but to turn the government over to his enemies.[9]

Grant manifested a similar reluctance to interfere in Alabama, but the situation degenerated so quickly that he had no choice but to become involved. Republicans elected the governor there in the 1872 elections. Both Conservatives and Republicans claimed victory in several disputed state legislative races. Whichever party's candidates were seated in those disputes would control the legislature. Conservatives quickly took possession of the capitol and seated Conservative claimants from the disputed districts. In response, the Republican legislators organized in the Montgomery federal courthouse and recognized *their* claimants. The new governor, David P. Lewis, recognized the Republican body, and when the Conservatives called for the aid of the white state militia, Lewis persuaded the local federal military garrison to station troops around the courthouse to prevent bloodshed. In response to Lewis's call for support, Grant could recognize the Republican government and order the national troops to install it in the capitol, or he could withdraw the troops as Conservatives and Democrats were demanding and permit a state civil war or a Republican surrender. Instead, he suggested a compromise that left the state house of representatives Republican and the state senate Conservative. Both sides accepted it, and Grant withdrew the troops. (By a shady parliamentary maneuver, however, Republicans later expelled a challenged Conservative senator, thus gaining control of both houses of the legislature.)

By 1874, Alabama Conservatives were determined to win control of the state at any cost (see Document 17). Where they could, they stuffed ballot boxes. They blacklisted employees who supported the Republican candidates, intimidated Republican speakers, and attended Republican meetings, filling the front row seats with sullen, armed men. The foremost historian of Reconstruction in Alabama, strongly sympathetic to the Conservatives and hostile to the Republicans, dismissed Republican charges of violence, but he recorded, "The whites had made up their minds, and the other side knew it, or rather felt it in the air, and were thereby intimidated. . . . The whites were determined to win, peaceably if possible, forcibly if necessary. The very determination made them inclined to peace as long as possible and made the opposite party cautious about giving causes for conflict"; or, as one Alabama Conservative told a black Republican campaign worker less elegantly, "You might as well quit. We have made up our minds to carry the state or kill half of you negroes on election day." [10]

The Conservatives won by fourteen thousand votes. Two years later, with Conservatives appointing the election officials, they won by a two to one margin. The Republicans have never since won another state election.

In Arkansas the collapse had its roots in the long rivalry between the state's first Republican governor, Powell Clayton, and more conservative Republican enemies led by Joseph Brooks. In 1872 Liberal Republicans, Democrats, and Brooks's supporters nominated Brooks on a platform of opposition to the state's disfranchisement laws. Clayton's regular Republican organization responded by also endorsing an end to disfranchisement and nominating a conservative Republican, Elisha Baxter, for governor. While Brooks's supporters did their best to win the election through violence as well as through legitimate campaign tactics, Baxter's Republican supporters controlled the election machinery. Although Brooks probably won more votes than Baxter, the Republicans rigged the returns to give their candidate a narrow victory.

When Brooks protested, threatening to seize the government by force if necessary, the conservative Baxter turned to the Democrats for support. Reiterating his opposition to disfranchisement, appointing Democrats to patronage positions, and forming a state militia commanded by Democratic officers, by mid-1873 he had turned complete control of the state over to the party that had opposed his election.

Meanwhile, Republicans, including even state officials elected with Baxter, rallied behind Brooks. Finally, in April, 1874, a state judge found that the 1872 returns were fraudulent and declared Brooks entitled to the governorship. He took the oath of office and moved into the governor's office, state officers and the state supreme court recognized him, and his supporters seized the state armory and fortified the capitol, while he called on Grant for military support. Like Davis, Brooks cited the national government's obligation to protect states from domestic violence. But Baxter too called on Grant for aid, as Democrats rallied to his support. By May, two small armies faced each other in Little Rock with a detachment of United States troops in between, keeping the precarious peace.

Again unwilling to impose a state government on a state by his decision, Grant tried to fashion a compromise, urging both sides to turn the question over to the Democratic-controlled legislature (*Alternative 5:* see Document 18). But that meant certain defeat for Brooks, who insisted that he would abide only by the decision of the state's Republican supreme court. To the dismay of radical Republicans, Grant then recognized Baxter and commanded Brooks's army to disband, leaving the state in Democratic hands. Holding control of the legislature, the Democrats, with Baxter's support, called a new constitutional convention which abrogated the Republican constitution of 1868 and vacated key state offices held by Republicans. Democrats were elected in their stead. This was too much even for Grant, who now conceded the validity of Brooks's claims and denounced the Democrats' "violence, intimidation, and revolutionary proceedings." [11] But he was still unwilling to interfere personally and in 1875 merely referred the matter to Congress.

Crisis in Louisiana

Bad as conditions were in Arkansas and Alabama, matters were still worse in Louisiana, the only state where national Republicans intervened on behalf of their southern allies.

Once again, the state crisis originated in factional disputes among Republicans. Republican Governor Henry Clay Warmoth, who had moved to Louisiana only in 1865, slowly lost control of the party machinery to opponents whose power lay in their control of the national patronage. Unable to shake his adversaries' influence with Grant, Warmoth allied with the Liberal Republican movement despite his own shady record. In 1872 his followers coalesced with Democrats to support a joint state ticket, nominating Democrat John McEnery for governor and a white Warmoth-supporter for lieutenant governor, while Republicans supported Senator William P. Kellogg for the governorship. With Warmoth's henchmen controlling the election machinery, there was so much fraud that it is impossible to this day to tell who actually won. But the new state constitution entrusted the counting and verifying of the results to an election board made up of the governor, lieutenant governor, secretary of state and two state senators, of whom only Warmoth supported the Democratic-Liberal Republican ticket. However, since the lieutenant governor and senator had been candidates in the election, they resigned, leaving their places to be filled by the remaining three. Warmoth nominated two of his allies, while the Republican secretary of state and remaining state senator nominated two of theirs. But Warmoth then suspended the secretary of state on a technicality and named one of his friends as a replacement. They then filled the two remaining vacancies with Warmoth's nominees, giving the Liberals and Democrats control of the board.

In response to this blatant fraud, the former secretary of state and the last regular Republican board member withdrew, elected *their* nominees to the two vacancies, and asked Warmoth to join them. When he refused, they claimed to constitute the legitimate board. As the Warmoth board, which had the official returns, counted in the Democratic-Liberal Republican candidates for governor and the state legislature, the Republican board, doing the best it could without the official records, declared the Republican candidates elected. Both sides appealed to allies in the state and federal courts; both won judgments in their favor. By January, 1873 there were two state governments and legislatures in New Orleans, one with McEnery at its head and the other with Kellogg. Both groups appealed to Grant for recognition as the true government of the state, which the national government would have to sustain against insurrection. Grant reluctantly recognized the Republican regime, but he ordered national troops to protect each government from attack by the other. Not wishing to be the final arbiter, he hoped the rival organizations would seek a judicial determination of the question. Fearing that they would not, he urged Congress to take some action to relieve him of the responsibility.

Congressional Republicans could not agree on what to do. Democrats and the most conservative Republicans wanted Grant simply to withdraw all federal troops, and let the Democrats sweep away the Republican government by force. Most moderate Republicans and Grant wanted Congress to order new elections, with Warmoth remaining in office until they were held. But radicals protested vehemently against keeping Warmoth in office, knowing that he would use his power to secure a Democratic victory in the new campaign. Fragmented in three directions, fearing criticism no matter what they did, congressional Republicans refused to act at all, leaving the mess in Grant's hands. Unhappily, Grant notified Kellogg that "any compromise that will suit all parties in Louisiana will suit the President." [12]

In March, 1873, a mob of McEnery supporters attacked the New Orleans police stations. Federal troops, following Grant's orders not to permit either side to attack the other, came to the policemen's aid. The mob was repulsed in a bloody battle, and the police, with the acquiescence of the federal troops, finally arrested and dispersed the McEnery legislature, leaving Kellog fully in control of the government.

Convinced that they had been deprived of victory through fraud and federal interference, Democrats prepared to seize the government by force. They organized armed "White Leagues," which drilled and paraded, promising not to begin bloodshed but vowing, in the words of a Democratic newspaper, that "if a single hostile gun is fired between the white and blacks, every carpet-bagger and scalawag that can be caught will in twelve hours be hanging from a limb." [13]

As the White Leagues spread from Louisiana to Mississippi and other southern states, Grant finally ended his passivity. Orders from the Justice and War departments instructed United States marshals to preserve the peace and protect citizens' rights during the campaign of 1874. National military officers were told to put their troops at the federal officials' disposal, to station them near polling places where violence threatened, and to help arrest offenders if the civilian law enforcement officers were defied.

But there were only about three thousand troops in the entire South. About one thousand of these were sent to eight stations in Louisiana; another six hundred were placed in ten strategic locations in South Carolina. The rest were scattered. Naturally, the puny bands of troops were ineffectual. They could not respond quickly or powerfully enough to prevent intimidation or even massacres like the coldblooded murder of six Republican officials in Coushatta, Louisiana, the killing of twenty-nine blacks in Vicksburg, Mississippi, or election day riots in Mobile and Eufala, Alabama.

The most serious threat to governmental authority came from the White Leagues' original home in Louisiana. In September, 1874, New Orleans residents drove the state police into the hastily barricaded statehouse and the United States custom house in a bloody battle that left over fifty people dead. Within a day the police and the black state militia units in the city surrendered. The mob, proclaiming McEnery the rightful governor of the state, took possession of the capitol and all the state property, while Kellogg fled to the custom house. Throughout the state, the Democratic-Liberal Republican candidates of 1872 seized power from their Republican rivals.

As Kellogg desperately wired Grant for military help, white Louisiana civic groups, business organizations, and leaders urged the president to recognize the leaders of the coup. But Grant was finally exasperated with southern violence. He delayed two days and then instructed the local federal garrison to suppress the rebellion. The coup collapsed, McEnery's forces surrendered their captured state property, and Kellogg returned to his office. However, the McEnery officers were slower to give up office in rural areas, where White Leaguers continued to ride, and in the fall, 1874 elections, held just a month and a half after the attempted coup, Democrats were sure that they had carried the state. But Republicans were unwilling to concede a victory that they were certain was due to the White Leagues' intimidation. The ubiquitous election board was again called into action; it proclaimed the election of an equal number of Democrats and Republicans to the state house of representatives, leaving five disputed seats to be decided by the equally divided body.

Once again Louisiana careened towards civil war. When the new state legislature met in January, 1875, the Democrats were in a minority, but they moved the election of a new speaker. Before the vote could be taken, their candidate seized the speaker's chair and gavel. Then, in the wild confusion, ignoring Republican shouts and objections, he declared Democratic candidates elected clerk and sergeant at arms. Suddenly, men who had forced their way into the chamber turned down the lapels of their suits, displaying blue badges marked "assistant sergeant at arms," and began throwing out the former house officers. Republicans struggled to leave in order to deprive the Democrats of the quorum necessary to proceed, but the assistant sergeants held five men down by force. The Democrats then settled the five disputed seats in favor of their allies, establishing their majority.

It was another coup d'état responding to another fraud, which in turn had been the response to more violence. Once more Kellogg appealed to the federal military garrison. The Republican legislators returned to the statehouse accompanied by soldiers, who forced the five challenged Democrats from their seats. With this, the rest of the Democrats withdrew in protest.

The conflict in Louisiana had arrived at its logical conclusion. Although it was supported by the black half of Louisiana's population, the Republican state government depended for its survival on national military force alone. Soldiers had broken into a state legislative assembly and purged it. Democrats and many conservative Republicans assailed Grant for permitting such an outrage; Republicans assailed Louisiana Democrats for precipitating it. Almost pathetically Grant told Congress, "I have deplored the necessity which seemed to make it my duty under the Constitution and laws to direct such interference. I have always refused except where it seemed to be my imperative duty to act in such a manner. I have repeatedly and earnestly entreated the people of the South to live together in peace . . . ."[14]

But, blaming each other, both sides ignored the truth. By 1875 it was irrelevant to speak in terms of democracy in discussing Louisiana. Louisianans were at war, and only slightly more openly than the citizens of the rest of the South. Northern Republicans now faced their ultimate dilemma—having prematurely restored the southern states to the Union, they could now follow the alternative policy of protecting southern Republicans' right to participate freely in political life only through measures incompatible with democracy and federalism.

A Strategy of Noninterference

Republicans also faced a *political* dilemma. As they had expected, the 1874 congressional elections were a disaster. Stunned by scandals in their party and pinched by an economic recession, demoralized Republicans stayed home on election day while liberals and reformers voted the Democratic ticket. The House of Representatives went from two to one Republican to nearly two to one Democratic, although Republicans retained control of the Senate.

Continued military support for southern regimes believed to be corrupt by most Americans was not acceptable to the growing reform elements of the party. In the lame-duck session of Congress, meeting between the 1874 elections and the installation of the new congressmen, Garfield, Dawes, and other conservative Republicans opposed a new, draconian Force Act to prevent violence in the South. Although the radical Butler rallied the overwhelming majority of House Republicans to its support, the Senate did not consider it. (The lame-duck Congress did pass Sumner's Civil Rights Act, however, in part as a memorial to the great senator, who had died in 1874; the Supreme Court later ruled it unconstitutional.)

Yet, to the surprise of many leaders, the party rank and file reacted with tremendous enthusiasm to Grant's vigorous action in Louisiana in 1875. As Republicans sought to rebuild the party's strength in the North during the elections held in most states in 1875, they emphasized repeatedly the danger of turning the national government over to a party which owed its success to fraud and violence and insisted that southern Democrats who negated the fruits of the Union victory in the South could not be considered truly loyal. Democrats attacked them for "waving the bloody shirt" (see Document 19), but the Republicans began to reverse their defeats. In 1876 they took their political offensive to Congress, moving to exclude Jefferson Davis from a new Democratic Amnesty Act designed to restore officeholding privileges to the few ex-Confederates left out of the 1872 bill. Republican support in the North continued to solidify as Democrats defended the symbol of the South's treason.

But while Republicans wrung political profits from the Democratic outrages in the South, they did little to stop them. In the state election of 1875, Mississippi whites formulated the "Mississippi Plan," adapting the tactic of organized intimidation used so successfully in Alabama in 1874. The election is remembered as the "Revolution of 1875" (see Document 20). Democrats drew the "white line," which meant that every white man not enrolled in local Democratic clubs was ostracized, vilified, or worse. Younger Democrats were organized into uniformed, semimilitary units, generally commanded by former Confederate officers. Armed men attended Republican political meetings and demanded the right to answer Republican speakers. Blacks were warned of the consequences of a Republican victory. But when Governor Ames called for national help, Grant—burned by his Louisiana experience—wrote his attorney general that "the whole public are tired out with these annual autumnal outbreaks in the South and the great majority are ready now to condemn any interference on the part of the government."[15]

Assured by leading Mississippi Democrats and Ames's Republican enemies that there would be no violence, Grant maintained his position until the intimidation became too blatant to ignore. Just as he was reconsidering his decision, Blaine, Garfield, and other conservative Republican leaders warned him not to risk the northern elections by taking action, and the Mississippi Republicans were allowed to go under in what a historian has recently called "the most degrading election in the history of the American republic."[16] Once again Democrats began impeachment proceedings against a Republican governor, and bowing to the inevitable, Ames resigned. Radical Republicans like Ben Butler, Ames's father-in-law, watched in frustrated impotence.

By 1875, conservative Republicans had solved their political dilemma in the North. They would maintain the enthusiasm of the Republican rank and file by vigorously assailing Democratic tactics in the South, while refusing actually to intervene on behalf of their southern allies, thus avoiding the alienation of liberals and reformers. In the presidential campaign of 1876, Republicans continued to apply the strategy. "Our strong ground is the dread of a solid South, rebel rule, etc., etc. ... It leads people away from 'hard times,' which is our deadliest foe," the Republican candidate, Rutherford B. Hayes, wrote Blaine. But when it came to action, he told Carl Schurz, a bitter Liberal Republican critic of military intervention, that he "substantially agreed" with Schurz's insistence that "the constitutional rights of local self-government must be respected." And publicly he announced that the southern states' "first necessity is an intelligent and honest administration of government .... What the South most needs is 'peace'...." Although he also affirmed that those governments ought to "protect all classes of citizens in their ... rights," the statement was clearly a slap at the "corrupt" carpetbaggers and scalawags and a bid for Liberal Republican support.[17]

The conservative Republican strategy of "all talk, no action," illustrated in their acquiescence in the Mississippi outrage, virtually invited whites to overthrow the last remaining Republican southern state governments in Louisiana, Florida, and South Carolina during the 1876 elections. At least to some extent the invitation was accepted. William A. Dunning, an early historian of Reconstruction and no friend of the Republicans, wrote that "the 'Mississippi plan' was enthusiastically applied in the ... three states ... in the elections of 1876."[18] Later historians have been less certain of the extent of the fraud and violence.

Louisiana had the most peaceful election, although Republicans alleged some violence (but the *threat* of violence may have been as effective as its use, as southerners had learned from Alabama's 1874 experience). In Florida the intimidation was well organized and consisted largely of economic rather than physical reprisals. The Democratic candidate for governor in South Carolina, Wade Hampton, appealed for blacks' support and promised to maintain their rights, while his party organized into military companies, broke up Republican meetings, and threatened Republican voters ("It was generally believed that nothing but bloodshed and a good deal of it could answer the purpose of redeeming the state," South Carolina Senator "Pitchfork" Ben Tillman remembered in later years).[19]

In the past, Louisiana Republicans had reacted to Democratic violence and fraud by having the Republican-dominated election board throw out disputed returns, and the machinery existed for South Carolina and Florida to follow the example. But after the Mississippi debacle, there seemed no longer to be any guarantee that the national government would sustain Republican governments elected in that way. It is possible that southern Republicans would have acquiesced when the raw returns showed narrow Democratic victories in all three state races and in two of the three states' presidential canvasses (Hayes carried South Carolina, even though the Republican state candidates seemed to have lost). But the state results took on national implications. Based on the returns from all the other states, the Democratic candidate, Samuel J. Tilden, was only one electoral vote short of victory. If the Republican election boards of the three states followed the Louisiana precedent and converted the fraudulent Democratic victories into fraudulent Republican ones, Hayes would win the election by one electoral vote.

Suddenly, radicals' fears that their failure to rescue their southern allies might wreck Republicans' national power seemed to be coming true. Sadly, Republicans pondered the implications for southern loyalists. Hayes wrote in his diary, "Both of us [Hayes and his wife] felt more anxiety about the South—about the colored people especially than about anything else . . . in the results." Zachariah Chandler, serving as the party's national chairman, worried that "in most parts of the South republicans would hardly be able to live if Tilden should be elected . . . ." And it seemed so blatantly unfair! "History will hold that the Republicans were by fraud and violence and intimidation, by a nullification of the 15th amendment, deprived of the victory which they fairly won," Hayes bitterly confided to his diary.[20]

Convinced that "the Democrats have carried no less than six states by fraud or intimidation," Washington campaign organizers wired the southern Republican state officials: "Hayes is elected if we have carried South Carolina, Florida, and Louisiana. Can you hold your State?"[21] It was what many of the southerners had been hoping for. With national party support, they turned to their Republican-dominated election boards to remedy the frauds that they were so certain had cost them their elections.

Democrats protested wildly. Quickly, they appointed eminent leaders to go South to make sure the votes were counted fairly. Republicans in turn sent their representatives. "Do not allow our folks to be bulldozed," the radical Chandler instructed one of them. "We have had enough of that."[22] Fortified by outside moral, political, and in some cases financial support, in all three states the Republican election boards announced Republican state and national victories and certified Republicans to cast their state's votes in the electoral college. The furious Democrats refused to abide by the decisions, and their electors also sent their votes to Washington. At the same time, both sides claimed victory in the state elections. Once again each side appealed to friendly courts, and by January, 1877, Louisiana and South Carolina each had rival governors and state legislatures. Once more both sides began to arm.* Northerners who came to the South in an effort to uncover the truth discovered the inappropriateness of the search where politics had taken on life and death meaning. "It is terrible to see the extent to which all classes go

*In Florida, the state supreme court at the request of the Democratic candidate for governor, ruled that the state election board had no power to investigate the accuracy of the raw election returns. Grudgingly, the board obeyed the court's order to recount all the ballots and declared the Democrat the winner by 200 votes. At first Republicans threatened to disrupt the new governor's inauguration, but when the Democrats brought in reinforcements from the country-side, they abandoned the fight. (The court's decision could not affect the votes of the presidential electors; the Constitution gives the right to canvass the electoral vote to Congress alone, and it would have to decide between the Democratic and Republican electors.)

in their determination to win," one of them wrote home. "Conscience offers no restraint. Nothing is so common as the resort to perjury, unless it is violence—in short, I do not know whom to believe."[23]

The Struggle Becomes National: Deciding the Presidential Election

The political chaos of the South had infected the nation. The Constitution requires the presiding officer of the Senate to announce each state's electoral vote in the presence of both houses of Congress. During the Civil War, Congress had passed resolutions providing a system for adjudicating disputes over challenged electoral votes, but they had been repealed, and a year earlier the Democratic House had refused to agree to a new resolution passed by the Republican Senate. In the absence of such a resolution, Republicans now argued, the president *pro tempore* of the Senate, Republican Thomas W. Ferry, would have to decide which votes to count from the three southern states. But Democrats denied that the framers of the Constitution had intended to put such power into the hands of one man. Somehow, both houses of Congress must participate in the decision, they insisted, and if no agreement could be reached, as was likely since Republicans controlled the Senate while Democrats controlled the House, then the challenged state's electoral votes should not be counted for either side. In that case, neither candidate would win a majority of the votes cast in the electoral college and under the Constitution, it would be left to the House of Representatives to choose the new president. With the Democrats' overwhelming majority there, there could be little doubt who that would be.

At first, neither party would give an inch. Democrats insisted that they would not permit the House to participate in counting the electoral vote unless Republicans gave in; Republicans threatened to go on without them and have Ferry count in Hayes. But House Democrats might counter by claiming that the count was illegal and that therefore no candidate had received the necessary majority of votes in the Electoral College. Then they might proceed to have the House elect Tilden. There would be two presidents, possibly even two Congresses, each recognizing one or the other.

But with Grant lame-duck president, Republicans had control of the armed forces, and this left the Democrats in a weak position. To make their challenge effective, they would have to resort to force, and most of them were unwilling to take this step. Yet the Republicans' position was not enviable. Many moderate leaders feared that a partisan victory, based primarily on force, might mean disaster in future elections. From over the country individuals and organizations called on Congress to agree to some compromise proposal.

Moreover, some Republican Senators were beginning to balk at insisting that their presiding officer alone should count the votes. One of the most influential Republicans in the Senate, New York's Roscoe Conkling, who feared Hayes would turn his state's patronage over to rivals in the party, announced his conviction that the House must participate in any decision. Another conservative, George F. Edmunds, urged that the votes be referred to members of the Supreme Court. At last, conservative and moderate Republican senators, over the objections of their candidate and radicals, joined the Democrats to create a special commission empowered to decide which votes from Florida, Louisiana, and South Carolina should be counted and to report its decision back to Congress. The commission decision would be binding unless *both* houses voted to overturn it. House Democrats, certain of the strength of their case and fearing that Tilden could be inaugurated no other way, agreed to the commission despite the misgivings of Tilden and the opposition of a few of the most extreme members of their own party.

The electoral commission was to consist of five representatives and five senators, with the parties evenly balanced, and five justices of the Supreme Court. Two of the latter were Democrats and two were Republicans and these four were to pick the fifth. Observers expected that they would choose Justice David Davis, a political independent with somewhat closer ties to Democrats than to Republicans. But just before the electoral commission resolution passed, Illinois Democrats joined Greenbackers (an independent party) to elect Davis to the Senate. His nonpartisanship now in question, Davis declined to participate on the commission, and instead the four justices chose Joseph Bradley, a conservative Republican.

The charges and countercharges of fraud and violence were far too complex to be investigated in the short time remaining before a new president had to be inaugurated. Moreover, the commissioners must have known that there would be no way to get at the truth. The eight Republican members, therefore, decided that the correct procedure was simply to accept the votes of presidential electors who had been officially designated by the recognized state governments; that is, the Republicans. The seven Democratic members protested, but they did not propose to find out the truth either. All they wanted to do was to accept at face value the raw election returns, without going behind them to learn what effect fraud and violence might have had on the vote.

It was a partisan vote (although all the commission members naturally denied that they were motivated by partisanship), but there was little the Democrats could do. Some of them wanted to prevent the count from proceeding at all, but others asked what good that would do? If Grant's term expired before a successor were inaugurated, either he would hold over as a sort of caretaker, or—more likely—the man next in line in case of the incapacity of the president and vice-president would take over. That man was the president *pro tempore* of the Senate, the Republican Ferry.

In the uncertainty, Democratic unity broke down. The majority wanted to make at least some token opposition. All agreed to vote against the commission recommendations, despite their earlier promise to abide by them. But a protest vote would accomplish little, because the resolution required the counting of the Republican votes unless *both* branches of Congress voted to replace them with the Democratic ballots. Most Democrats decided on at least a token filibuster in the joint meeting of Congress called to count the electoral votes, recognizing at the same time that the cause was finally lost.

Meanwhile, Republicans were faced again with trouble in the South. Grant, absolutely sick of the everlasting southern crises, refused to recognize any of the governments in Louisiana and South Carolina, only ordering United States forces there to prevent aggression on either side. Protected by the troops, the Republican governors and legislatures controlled the state-houses, while Democratic candidates took over offices in the rest of each state. In the first days of his new administration, Hayes would have to decide whether to incur the negative reaction which greeted Grant's intervention to help the Louisiana Republicans, or let the last southern Republican governments fall.

Conciliation

It was precisely in order to succor southern Republicans that so many rank and file Republicans had urged a firm stand on Hayes's inauguration. But some of the candidate's closest advisers, especially Carl Schurz, Garfield, Senator John Sherman, Ohio ex-Governor Jacob D. Cox, and influential Ohio Republican Stanley Matthews, had long agreed with conservative southern Republicans that the only hope for building a strong party there lay in appealing to whites. Other agents told Hayes that many former southern Whigs and anti-secessionists of 1861 were again expressing dissatisfaction with their Democratic allies. If the Republican party would only discard its radical southern element, these dissident Conservatives would gravitate to the Republicans on new issues, Hayes's informants assured him. Republicans should try conciliation again, they insisted. By centering their appeal on the protective tariff and government aid to southern transportation companies, muting their defense of southern loyalists' rights, they would precipitate a realignment of parties in the South and in the long run do more to protect those rights than all the troops in the country. Sensing northern impatience with the old Republican programs, convinced that the alternatives of national protection and internal reconstruction of political power based on black votes had failed, Hayes prepared to launch a new southern policy.

With Hayes already leaning to the new policy, Louisiana Democrats decided to try to commit him to recognizing their state government. Warning that Democrats would carry out their threat to filibuster the joint meeting of Congress called to count the electoral votes unless Hayes clarified his position on the southern contested state elections, they forced Hayes's hand. At a secret meeting at the Wormley House hotel, Hayes's intimates promised South Carolina and Louisiana representatives that he would withdraw the national troops from the state capitals, while Democrats promised not to abridge black southerners' right to vote.

A little over a year later, the chief Louisiana Democratic negotiator acknowledged that the threat "had been a bluff game." Whether or not Hayes had acceded to the southern demands, he admitted, "I think the count would have been terminated."[24]

On the other hand, the Democrats had only committed Hayes to doing what he and conservative Republicans had wanted to do all along. Weeks before the Wormley conference, Cox had written, "The lapse of time has so far consolidated and established the political rights of the Negroes that their separate organization as a party is no longer essential to their safety. On the contrary, it is now the cause of their greatest danger." With Democrats promising "that they will in honorable good faith accept & defend the present Constitutional rights of the freedman, we ought not to have great difficulty in finding means to rally to the support of a Republican administration a strong body of the best men . . . of the South, willing to cooperate in the good work of bringing in an era of real peace, prosperity & good brotherhood."[25] Hayes had answered, "Your views and mine are so precisely the same that if called on to write down a policy I could adopt your language."[26] Called upon to promulgate a policy; Hayes adopted Cox's language (*Alternative 5: see* Document 21). Hayes was inaugurated on March 5, 1877. On April 10 and 24, respectively, United States troops returned to their barracks in South Carolina and Louisiana, and the last Republican governments of the South collapsed.[27]

Notes

1. *Congressional Globe*, 42d Cong., 2d sess., May 21, 1872, p. 2824.

2. James D. Richardson, comp., *A Compilation of the Messages and Papers of the Presidents* . . . (New York, 1897), vol. 9, pp. 4153-54.

3. Attorney General George H. Williams to David T. Corbin (U.S. District Attorney, South Carolina), Dec. 7, 1872, Department of Justice Instruction Books, Record Group 60, National Archives, Washington, D.C.

4. Silas F. Smith to Ulysses S. Grant, Jan. 13, 1873, Department of Justice Letters Received (President), Record Group 60, National Archives.

5. John A. Minnis (U.S. District Attorney, Middle District Alabama) to Williams, Jan. 20, 1873, Department of Justice Letters Received, Record Group 60, National Archives.

6. Garfield to Burke A. Hinsdale, Dec. 13, 1872, in *Garfield-Hinsdale Letters: Correspondence Between James Abram Garfield and Burke Aaron Hinsdale*, ed. Mary L. Hinsdale (Ann Arbor, Michigan: University of Michigan Press, 1949), p. 202.

7. Charles William Ramsdell, *Reconstruction in Texas* (New York: Longmans, Green & Co., 1910), p. 315.

8. Thomas F. Purnell to Grant, Jan. 12, 1874 in *A Hand-Book of Politics for 1874* . . ., ed. Edward McPherson (Washington, D.C., 1874), p. 109.

9. Williams to Davis, Jan. 17, 1874, and Davis to Williams, Jan. 19, 1874, in ibid., p. 111.

10. Walter L. Fleming, *Civil War and Reconstruction in Alabama* (New York: Columbia University Press, 1905), pp. 791-92.

11. Richardson, comp., *Messages and Papers of the Presidents*, vol. 9, p. 4273.

12. Williams to Kellogg, Mar. 5, 1873, Department of Justice Letterbooks, Record Group 60, National Archives.

13. Ella Lonn, *Reconstruction in Louisiana After 1868* (New York: G.P. Putnam's Sons, 1918), p. 258.

14. Richardson, comp., *Messages and Papers of the Presidents*, vol. 9, p. 4267.

15. Attorney General Edwards Pierrepont to Ames, Sept. 14, 1875, *A Hand-Book of Politics for 1876*, ed. Edward McPherson, p. 42.

16. Keith Ian Polokoff, *The Politics of Intertia: The Election of 1876 and the End of Reconstruction* (Baton Rouge, University of Louisiana Press, 1973), p. 180.

17. Hayes to Blaine, Sept. 14, 1876, quoted in James Ford Rhodes, *History of the United States From the Compromise of 1850 to the Final Restoration of Home Rule at the South in 1877*, 7 vols. (New York: Macmillan Co., 1906), vol. 7, p. 220; Schurz to Hayes, June 21, 1876, Hayes Mss., Rutherford B. Hayes Library, Fremont, Ohio; Hayes to Schurz, June 27, 1876. Schurz Mss., Library of Congress; McPherson, ed., *Hand-Book of Politics for 1876*, p. 213.

18. William A. Dunning, "The Undoing of Reconstruction," *Atlantic Monthly*, vol. 88 (October, 1901), p. 441.

19. Francis Butler Simkins and Robert Hilliard Woody, *South Carolina During Reconstruction* (Chapel Hill: University of North Carolina Press, 1932), p. 487.

20. T. Harry Williams, ed., *Hayes: The Diary of a President, 1875-1881, Covering the Disputed Election, the End of Reconstruction, and the Beginning of Civil Service* (New York: D. McKay Co., 1964), pp. 47-50; Chandler to J.H. White, Nov. 23, 1876, Papers of the Select House Committee on Powers of the House in Counting Electoral Votes, 44th Cong., Record Group 233, National Archives.

21. Chandler to W.F. Henderson, Dec. 9, 1876, Papers of the Select House Committee on Powers of the House, Record Group 233, National Archives, *New York Times*, June 15, 1887.

22. Chandler to Lew Wallace, Dec. 18, 1876, Papers of the Select House Committee on Powers of the House, Record Group 233 National Archives.

23. Lew Wallace, *Lew Wallace: An Autobiography* 2 vols. (New York: Harper & Bros., 1906), vol. 2, pp. 901-902.

24. *House Miscellaneous Document Number 31*, 45th Cong., 3d sess., vol. 1, p. 990.

25. Cox to Hayes, Jan. 31, 1877, Hayes Mss., Hayes Memorial Library, Fremont, Ohio.

26. Hayes to Cox, Feb. 2, 1877, Cox Mss., Oberlin College Archives, Oberlin, Ohio.

27. In this account of the so-called Compromise of 1877 I have minimized the importance of the railroad lobby in the adjustment. Students should know that some historians believe that there was an economic side to the compromise too. I discuss that question more fully in the bibliographic essay.

Epilogue

In 1878, William Henry Smith, Hayes's closest political adviser, insisted that "it is only a question of time when there will arise a really Republican party in the South numbering in its ranks the intelligence, the culture, the wealth, the Protestantism of the Southern white people, who will give protection and support to the colored people in their midst."[1] But by the end of that year it was clear to all that conciliation had even more dismally failed to secure the rights of southern loyalists than the earlier Republican alternatives. Democratic southern state legislatures changed the laws governing landlord-tenant relations, putting sharecroppers at the mercy of landowners; black craftsmen were forced from their professions; crimes against black people went unpunished; taxes went to support white rather than black schools. Republicans' right to vote became more tightly circumscribed than it had been before, without even the semblance of state protection, and the national government was no longer willing or able to send troops to guarantee fair elections. In the 1878 elections Republican congressional candidates in South Carolina received only four-thousand votes compared to ninety-thousand two years earlier. Throughout the deep South, the Republican party virtually ceased to exist except as a skeleton organization of national office holders.

From 1879 through the 1880s, Republican leaders continued to assail racial repression in the South, but as time went on their complaints took a progressively more political cast. While they remained concerned about black people's rights, Republicans expended more effort trying to rebuild their political organization in the South than succoring the freedmen. Republican leaders tried to fashion alliances with insurgent Democrats and to foster all-white Republican party organizations to escape the taint of racial liberalism. But nothing worked. The "Solid South" remained solidly Democratic, solidly racist.

Finally, in 1890 Republicans turned a last time to the alternative of national protection. Two veterans of Reconstruction, Senators George F. Hoar and George F. Edmunds, and Representative Henry Cabot Lodge, whose father was one of Sumner's close friends, proposed a new Election bill that would have placed congressional and presidential elections under complete national supervision wherever one hundred citizens of a congressional district asked for national aid. For a year the debate over the Election bill refired the passions of the Reconstruction era, but in the end, the bill failed to pass, killed by popular reluctance to reopen old wounds and by the fears of northern Republican businessmen that sectional strife would inhibit trade with the South.

The Election bill was the last Republican effort to secure some measure of what their predecessors of 1865 had believed to be the fruits of victory. Strong elements of the party remained sympathetic to black southerners' plight well into the twentieth century, as white southerners disfranchised them and created a rigid state-enforced system of racial discrimination and segregation. But northerners attempted no legislative remedies. The battle was ended.

Notes

1. Smith to A.C. McClurg, Aug. 23, 1878, William Henry Smith Mss., Ohio State Historical Society, Columbus, Ohio.

Part two ⸺⸺⸺⸺

⸺⸺⸺ Documents
of the
Decision

1

Southern White Attitudes Towards the Freedmen as Workers

Sidney Andrews and John R. Dennett were among the most acute observers who reported on conditions in the South in 1865 and 1866. Later published in book form, Andrews's reports appeared originally in the Boston *Daily Advertiser* and the *Chicago Tribune*, while Dennett's were carried under the heading "The South As It Is" by the weekly newspaper, the New York *Nation.* The Freedmen's Bureau, mentioned in Dennett's account, was a semi-military bureau established in 1865 to aid in the transition from slave to free labor and to alleviate war-induced suffering in the South.

Document 1-a†

The "Character of the Negro"

Coming up in the cars from Charleston I had for seatmate part of the way one of the delegates to the Convention which meets at Columbia next week. He was a very courteous and agreeable gentleman, past middle age, and late the owner of twenty-two negroes. He was good enough to instruct me at some length in respect to the character of the negro. "You Northern people are utterly mistaken in supposing anything can be done with these negroes in a free condition. They can't be governed except with the whip. Now on my plantation there wasn't much whipping, say once a fortnight; but the negroes knew they would be whipped if they didn't behave themselves, and the fear of the lash kept them in good order." He went on to explain what a good home they always had; laying stress on the fact that they never were obliged to think for themselves, but were always tenderly cared for, both in health and sickness; "and yet these niggers all left me the day after the Federals got into Charleston!" I asked where they now are; and he replied that he hadn't seen anybody but his old cook since they ran away; but he believed they were all at work except two, who had died. Yet I am told constantly that these ungrateful wretches, the negroes, cannot possibly live as free people.

Yesterday morning while I sat in the office of the agent of the Freedmen's Bureau there came in, with a score of other men, a planter living in this

†From: Sidney Andrews, *The South Since the War* ... (Boston, 1866), pp. 25-26.

district, but some sixteen miles from town. He had a woful tale of an assault upon himself by one of his "niggers,"—"a boy who I broughten up, and who's allers had a good home down ter my place." While the boy was coming in from the street the man turned to me and explained, "It never don't do no good to show favor to a nigger, for they's the most ongratefullest creeturs in the world." The dreadful assault consisted in throwing a hatchet at the white man by one of a crowd of negroes who were having a dispute among themselves, and suddenly discovered, in the early evening, somebody sneaking along by the fence. The boy said it wasn't a hatchet, but a bit of brick; and added, that the man was so far away that no one could tell whether he was white or black, and that he didn't throw the brick till after he called out and told the man to go away. I followed the negro out after he had received his lecture from the officer, and had some talk with him. "D——n him," said he, referring to his employer, "he never done nufin all his d——n life but beat me and kick me and knock me down; an' I hopes I git eben with him some day."

Document 1-b†

White Expectations

"The Negro," said Mr. K——, "I sincerely hope may disappoint my expectations. But if he does not, he is doomed to undergo extinction. Less than a hundred years of freedom will see the race practically exterminated. The Negro will not work more than enough to supply his bare necessities. There isn't a county of Virginia where we haven't had some hundreds of free Negroes, and they have been always perfectly worthless and lived in wretchedness. The Negro stands as much in need of a master to guide him as a child does. When I look at my servants, I feel weighing upon me all the responsibilities of a parent. In the course of my life I have known many men who for that reason alone would never become the owner of a slave. I have brought up my children to feel so, and accustomed them to the thought of dispensing with slave labor. Those of them who are old enough share my views on the subject. But the Negro will always need the care of someone superior to him, and unless in one form or another it is extended to him, the race will first become pauper and then disappear. Nothing but the most careful legislation will prevent it. Now take an example: of my Negroes, nearly half were not on the working list; but I had to support them all. What will the Negro do when he is called upon to support not only himself (he isn't inclined to do that, and I don't believe he will do it), but also to get food, and clothes, and physic for the infants and disabled people belonging to him? Why, I doubt if my farm never returned me one per cent. interest on the capital invested in it. He cannot do it. He couldn't do it if all the Southern States were confiscated and given him to do it with. . . . "

The white people are often very far wrong in their notions of the object for which the Bureau of Freedmen was organized, and the power committed

†From: the New York *Nation,* July 27 and August 17, 1865.

to its officers. I was waiting the other day in the office of the superintendent when two gentlemen of respectable appearance entered and announced themselves as planters from the State of Mississippi. The conversation on their part was carried on by one, the other saying nothing. Both seemed to listen with very great interest to all that was said to them. The speaker said their business with the superintendent was to get from him about a hundred Virginia Negroes to be taken down to Mississippi to work on cotton. They were informed that the officer had no power to send away Negroes unless they chose to go. They asked if they couldn't get a hundred paupers or criminals. But the superintendent had not at command so many of either class or of both together. They asked if Negroes could not be apprenticed to them for a term of years. But apprenticeship, except of boys in cities, who in exceptional cases may be put with a tradesman to learn his craft, is not permitted.

"Well, now," said the gentleman, "this is how the thing is. I've got land there, and I'm going to raise cotton. I've spent pretty nearly $20,000 for mules and harnesses and a complete outfit generally. What I want to know is this—you say you can't use compulsion to make these Virginia niggers go down there—what compulsion will the Government let me use to make them work when I've got them there, anyhow?"

"You seem to think all Negro labor must be compulsory."

"Why, of course it must. How long have you lived in a slave State, sir?"

"I have lived within twenty-five miles of one a good part of my life. But you must look to the experience of those who have tried free labor. There is Mr. B. G——, on the James. He has about two hundred and eighty-seven Negroes. They were with him as slaves, and he has employed them all since they were emancipated. Only three went away from the place, and the rest, he says, are doing very well indeed. One example like that is worth a great deal of theory."

"Yes, I know him very well. Didn't know he had so many as that, though. But I know the nigger. The employer must have some sort of punishment. I don't care what it is. If you'll let me tie him up by the thumbs, or keep him on bread and water, that will do. Over here in Rockbridge County, as I came along I saw a nigger tied up by the wrists. His hands were away up above his head. I went along to him, and says I, 'Boy, which would you like best now, to stay there where you are, or to have me take you down, give you forty good cuts, and let you go?' 'Rather have the forty lash,' says he. So he would, too. You folks used to make a good deal of talk because we gave our niggers a flogging when they deserved it. I won't ask leave to flog, if you'll let me use some of your Northern punishments. All I want is just to have it so that when I get the niggers on to my place, and the work is begun, they can't sit down and look me square in the face and do nothing."

The superintendent could not encourage him to hope that the Bureau would deport Negroes to Mississippi, nor that it would allow him to use on his plantation the punishments which he seemed to think necessary.

2

The Sherman-Johnston Convention

Document†
2. The Confederate armies now in existence to be disbanded and conducted to the several State capitals, there to deposit their arms and public property in the State arsenal; and each officer and man to execute and file an agreement to cease from acts of war, and to abide the action of the State and Federal authority. . . .

3. The recognition by the Executive of the United States of the several State Governments, on their officers and Legislatures taking the oath prescribed by the Constitution of the United States, and, where conflicting State Governments have resulted from the war, the legitimacy of all shall be submitted to the Supreme Court of the United States. . . .

5. The people and inhabitants of all the States to be guaranteed, so far as the Executive can, their political rights and franchises, as well as their rights of person and property, as defined by the Constitution of the United States and of the States respectively.

6. The Executive authority of the Government of the United States not to disturb any of the people by reason of the late war so long as they live in peace and quiet, abstain from acts of armed hostility, and obey the laws in existence at the place of their residence.

7. In general terms the war to cease, a general amnesty, so far as the Executive of the United States can command, on condition of the disbandment of the Confederate armies, the distribution of the arms and the resumption of peaceful pursuits by the officers and men hitherto composing said armies.

†From: William T. Sherman, *Memoirs of General William T. Sherman,* 2 vols., 2d ed. (New York, 1887), vol. 2, pp. 356-57.

3

Presidential
Reconstruction

The Amnesty proclamation (Document 3-a) plus the North Carolina proclamation (Document 3-b), reprinted below, embodied the key elements of President Johnson's Reconstruction policy.

Document 3-a†

Amnesty Proclamation

... To the end that the authority of the Government of the United States may be restored and that peace, order, and freedom may be established, I, Andrew Johnson, President of the United States, do proclaim and declare that I hereby grant to all persons who have, directly or indirectly, participated in the existing rebellion, except as hereinafter excepted, amnesty and pardon, with restoration of all rights of property, except as to slaves, ... but upon the condition, nevertheless, that every such person shall take and subscribe the following oath (or affirmation) and thenceforward keep and maintain said oath inviolate, ... to wit:

I, ———, do solemnly swear (or affirm), in presence of Almighty God, that I will henceforth faithfully support, protect, and defend the Constitution of the United States and the Union of the States thereunder, and that I will in like manner abide by and faithfully support all laws and proclamations which have been made during the existing rebellion with reference to the emancipation of slaves. So help me God.

The following classes of persons are excepted from the benefits of this proclamation:

First. All who are or shall have been pretended civil or diplomatic officers or otherwise domestic or foreign agents of the pretended Confederate government.

Second. All who left judicial stations under the United States to aid the rebellion.

Third. All who shall have been military or naval officers of said pretended Confederate government above the rank of colonel in the army or lieutenant in the navy.

Fourth. All who left seats in the Congress of the United States to aid the rebellion.

Fifth. All who resigned or tendered resignations of their commissions in the Army or Navy of the United States to evade duty in resisting the rebellion.

†From: James D. Richardson, comp., *Messages and Papers of the Presidents* ... , 20 vols. (New York, 1897), vol. 8, pp. 3508-10.

Sixth. All who have engaged in any way in treating otherwise than lawfully as prisoners of war persons found in the United States service as officers, soldiers, seamen, or in other capacities. . . .

Eighth. All military and naval officers in the rebel service who were educated by the Government in the Military Academy at West Point or the United States Naval Academy.

Ninth. All persons who held the pretended offices of governors of States in insurrection against the United States. . . .

Thirteenth. All persons who have voluntarily participated in said rebellion and the estimated value of whose taxable property is over $20,000. . . .

Provided, That special application may be made to the President for pardon by any person belonging to the excepted classes, and such clemency will be liberally extended as may be consistent with the facts of the case and the peace and dignity of the United States.

Document 3-b†

North Carolina Proclamation

[In succeeding proclamations the president extended these provisions to other rebel states where Reconstruction had not yet begun during the war.]

. . . Whereas the rebellion which has been waged by a portion of the people of the United States against the properly constituted authorities of the Government thereof in the most violent and revolting form, but whose organized and armed forces have now been almost entirely overcome, has in its revolutionary progress deprived the people of the State of North Carolina of all civil government; and

Whereas it becomes necessary and proper to carry out and enforce the obligations of the United States to the people of North Carolina in securing them in the enjoyment of a republican form of government:

Now, therefore, in obedience to the high and solemn duties imposed upon me by the Constitution of the United States and for the purpose of enabling the loyal people of said State to organize a State government whereby justice may be established, domestic tranquillity insured, and loyal citizens protected in all their rights of life, liberty, and property, I, Andrew Johnson, President of the United States and Commander in Chief of the Army and Navy of the United States, do hereby appoint William W. Holden provisional governor of the State of North Carolina, whose duty it shall be, at the earliest practicable period, to prescribe such rules and regulations as may be necessary and proper for convening a convention composed of delegates to be chosen by that portion of the people of said State who are loyal to the United States, and no others, for the purpose of altering or amending the constitution thereof, and with authority to exercise within the limits of said State all the powers necessary and proper to enable such loyal people of the State of North

†From: Ibid., pp. 3510-12.

Carolina to restore said State to its constitutional relations to the Federal Government and to present such a republican form of State government as will entitle the State to the guaranty of the United States therefor and its people to protection by the United States against invasion, insurrection, and domestic violence: *Provided,* That in any election that may be hereafter held for choosing delegates to any State convention as aforesaid no person shall be qualified as an elector or shall be eligible as a member of such convention unless he shall have previously taken and subscribed the oath of amnesty as set forth in the President's proclamation of May 29, A. D. 1865, and is a voter qualified as prescribed by the constitution and laws of the State of North Carolina in force immediately before the 20th day of May, A. D. 1861, the date of the so-called ordinance of secession; and the said convention, when convened, or the legislature that may be thereafter assembled, will prescribe the qualification of electors and the eligibility of persons to hold office under the constitution and laws of the State—a power the people of the several States composing the Federal Union have rightfully exercised from the origin of the Government to the present time.

And I do hereby direct—

First. That the military commander of the department and all officers and persons in the military and naval service aid and assist the said provisional governor in carrying into effect this proclamation. . . .

Second. That the Secretary of State proceed to put in force all laws of the United States the administration whereof belongs to the State Department applicable to the geographical limits aforesaid.

Third. That the Secretary of the Treasury proceed to nominate for appointment assessors of taxes and collectors of customs and internal revenue and such other officers of the Treasury Department as are authorized by law and put in execution the revenue laws of the United States within the geographical limits aforesaid. . . .

Fourth. That the Postmaster-General proceed to establish post-offices and post routes and put into execution the postal laws of the United States within the said State. . . .

Fifth. That the district judge for the judicial district in which North Carolina is included proceed to hold courts within said State in accordance with the provisions of the act of Congress. . . .

Sixth. That the Secretary of the Navy take possession of all public property belonging to the Navy Department within said geographical limits and put in operation all acts of Congress in relation to naval affairs having application to the said State.

Seventh. That the Secretary of the Interior put in force the laws relating to the Interior Department applicable to the geographical limits aforesaid.

4

The
Black Codes

Every southern state had to revise its laws in light of the changes inherent in the abolition of slavery. Most did this by modifying the "black codes" that had regulated the relatively small number of free black southerners before the war. The new black codes offered far greater civil liberty than blacks had held before the war. They recognized the binding legal effect of marriage, gave broader access to the courts than ever before, and instituted some basic protections in employer-employee relations. But nowhere did they provide equality before the law, and in many cases they instituted inequalities that shocked the northern conscience. Some examples follow:

Document 4-a†

Police Regulations of St. Landry Parish, Louisiana

[These ordinances governing freedmen were among the most stringent in the South.]

Sec. 1. *Be it ordained by the police jury of the parish of St. Landry,* That no negro shall be allowed to pass within the limits of said parish without special permit in writing from his employer. . . .

Sec. 2. . . . Every negro who shall be found absent from the residence of his employer after ten o'clock at night, without a written permit from his employer, shall pay a fine of five dollars, or in default thereof, shall be compelled to work five days on the public road, or suffer corporeal punishment as hereinafter provided.

Sec. 3. . . . No negro shall be permitted to rent or keep a house within said parish. Any negro violating this provision shall be immediately ejected and compelled to find an employer. . . .

Sec. 4. . . . Every negro is required to be in the regular service of some white person, or former owner, who shall be held responsible for the conduct of said negro. But said employer or former owner may permit said negro to hire his own time by special permission in writing, which permission shall not extend over seven days at any one time. . . .

Sec. 5. . . . No public meetings or congregations of negroes shall be allowed within said parish after sunset; but such public meetings and congregations may be held between the hours of sunrise and sunset, by the special permission in writing of the captain of patrol, within whose beat such meetings shall take place. This prohibition, however, is not to prevent negroes

†From: *Senate Executive Document No. 2,* 39th Cong., 1st sess., pp. 93-94.

from attending the usual church services, conducted by white ministers and priests. . . .

Sec. 6. . . . No negro shall be permitted to preach, exhort, or otherwise declaim to congregations of colored people, without a special permission in writing from the president of the policy jury. . . .

Sec. 7. . . . No negro who is not in the military service shall be allowed to carry fire-arms, or any kind of weapons, within the parish, without the special written permission of his employers, approved and indorsed by the nearest and most convenient chief of patrol. . . .

Sec. 8. . . . No negro shall sell, barter, or exchange any articles of merchandise or traffic within said parish without the special written permission of his employer, specifying the article of sale, barter or traffic. . . .

Document 4-b†

South Carolina Licensing Law

[Similar laws were passed in several southern states. They were designed to ease competition that white artisans feared from blacks trained in mechanical crafts as slaves. Of course, whites enforced the law and determined whether black applicants were "qualified" to pursue their trades.]

No person of color shall pursue or practice the art, trade or business of an artisan, mechanic or shopkeeper, or any other trade, employment or business (besides that of husbandry, or that of a servant under a contract for service or labor,) on his own account and for his own benefit, or in partnership with a white person, or as agent or servant of any person, until he shall have obtained a license therefor from the Judge of the District Court; which license shall be good for one year only. This license the Judge may grant upon petition of the applicant, and upon being satisfied of his skill and fitness, and of his good moral character, and upon payment, by the applicant, to the Clerk of the District Court, of one hundred dollars, if a shopkeeper or peddler, to be paid annually, and ten dollars, if a mechanic, artisan or to engage in any other trade, also to be paid annually: *Provided, however,* That upon complaint being made and proved to the District Judge of an abuse of such license he shall revoke the same: *and provided, also,* That no person of color shall practice any mechanical art or trade unless he shows that he has served an apprenticeship in such trade or art, or is now practicing such trade or art. . . .

†From: *South Carolina Statutes at Large*, vol. 13, pp. 269-299.

Document 4-c†

Vagrancy Laws

[Northerners and southern blacks suspected that "vagrancy" laws, passed in all the southern states, were designed to permit planters to intimidate blacks into working for low wages in serf-like conditions, or face the prospect of being bound over as vagrants to work for no wages at all. Observers charged that in some areas planters agreed not to hire workers under ordinary contracts, so that they would be charged with vagrancy and made to work for no more than the price of the fine. These concerns impelled General Alfred H. Terry to void a Virginia law similar to the one reprinted below. Of course, the laws were enforced upon blacks by whites. Sidney Andrews described their attitude in his *The South Since the War.*]

Sec. 2. . . . All freedmen, free negroes and mulattoes in this State, over the age of eighteen years, found on the second Monday in January, 1866, or thereafter, with no lawful employment or business, or found unlawfully assembling themselves together, either in the day or night time, and all white persons so assembling themselves with freedmen, free negroes or mulattoes, or usually associating with freedmen, free negroes or mulattoes, on terms of equality, or living in adultery or fornication with a freed woman, free negro or mulatto, shall be deemed vagrants, and on conviction thereof shall be fined in a sum not exceeding, in the case of a freedman, free negro, or mulatto, fifty dollars, and a white man two hundred dollars, and imprisoned at the discretion of the court, the free negro not exceeding ten days, and the white man not exceeding six months.

Sec. 5. . . . In case any freedman, free negro or mulatto shall fail for five days after the imposition of any fine or forfeiture upon him or her for violation of any of the provisions of this act to pay the same, that it shall be, and is hereby, made the duty of the sheriff of the proper county to hire out said freedman, free negro or mulatto, to any person who will, for the shortest period of service, pay said fine and forfeiture and all costs. . . .

Document 4-d‡

Voiding the Law in Virginia
General Orders—No. 4.

Headquarters, Department of Va.,
Richmond, *January* 24, 1866.

By a statute passed at the present session of the Legislature of Virginia, entitled "A bill providing for the punishment of vagrants," it is enacted, among other things, that any justice of the peace, upon the complaint of any

†From: *Laws of Mississippi, 1865*, pp. 90-92.
‡From: Edward McPherson, ed., *Political History of the United States During* . . . *Reconstruction*, 2d ed. (Washington, D.C., 1875), pp. 41-42.

one of certain officers therein named, may issue his warrant for the apprehension of any person alleged to be a vagrant and cause such person to be apprehended and brought before him; and that if upon due examination said justice of the peace shall find that such person is a vagrant within the definition of vagrancy contained in said statute, he shall issue his warrant, directing such person to be employed for a term not exceeding three months, and . . . hired out for the best wages which can be procured, his wages to be applied to the support of himself and his family. . . . Among those declared to be vagrants are all persons who, not having the wherewith to support their families, live idly and without employment, and refuse to work for the usual and common wages given to other laborers in the like work in the place where they are.

In many counties of this State meetings of employers have been held, and unjust and wrongful combinations have been entered into for the purpose of depressing the wages of the freedmen below the real value of their labor, far below the prices formerly paid to masters for labor performed by their slaves. By reason of these combinations wages utterly inadequate to the support of themselves and families have, in many places, become the usual and common wages of the freedmen. The effect of the statute in question will be, therefore, to compel the freedmen, under penalty of punishment as criminals, to accept and labor for the wages established by these combinations of employers. It places them wholly in the power of their employers, and it is easy to foresee that, even where no such combination now exists, the temptation to form they offered by the statute will be too strong to be resisted, and that such inadequate wages will become the common and usual wages throughout the State. The ultimate effect of the statute will be to reduce the freedmen to a condition of servitude worse than that from which they have been emancipated—a condition which will be slavery in all but its name.

It is therefore ordered that no magistrate, civil officer or other person shall in any way or manner apply or attempt to apply the provisions of said statute to any colored person in this department.

By command of Major General A. H. Terry.

Document 4-e†

Black and White Attitudes Towards the Laws

Three fourths of the people assume that the negro will not labor except on compulsion; and the whole struggle between the whites on the one hand and the blacks on the other hand is a struggle for and against compulsion. The negro insists, very blindly perhaps, that he shall be free to come and go when he pleases; the white insists that he shall only come and go at the pleasure of his employer. The whites seem wholly unable to comprehend that freedom for the negro means the same thing as freedom for them. They readily enough

†From: Sidney Andrews, *The South Since the War*, (Boston, 1886), p. 398.

admit that the government has made him free, but appear to believe that they still have the right to exercise over him the old control. It is partly their misfortune, and not wholly their fault, that they cannot understand the national intent as expressed in the Emancipation Proclamation and the Constitutional Amendment. I did not anywhere find a man who could see that laws should be applicable to all persons alike; and hence even the best men hold that each State must have a negro code. They acknowledge the overthrow of the special servitude of man to man, but seek through these codes to establish the general servitude of man to the Commonwealth. I had much talk with intelligent gentlemen in various sections, and particularly with such as I met during the Conventions at Columbia and Milledgeville, upon this subject, and found such a state of feeling as warrants little hope that the present generation of negroes will see the day in which their race shall be amendable only to such laws as apply to the whites.

5

Radicals on Reconstruction 1865-1866

While Republican conservatives and moderates agreed fairly well on the key elements of their Reconstruction policy, radicals' views diverged more widely. All agreed that the freedmen had to be guaranteed the right to vote; nearly all wanted to replace the state governments created by President Johnson with territorial governments under congressional supervision. Some advocated guaranteed equal education; others urged confiscation and land redistribution; yet others stringent punishment of the leading traitors. Here are some of their proposals and justifications for them.

Document 5-a†

Resolutions of Charles Sumner

[Sumner offered these resolutions in the Senate on December 4, 1865. Beneath the verbiage, note the key conditions—"complete reestablishment of loyalty," black enfranchisement, repudiation of the rebel debt and confirmation of the national debt, equal education, the implied disqualification of former rebels from office, and the final, key resolution that restoration must be a slow process, implying some sort of long-term congressional control of the South.]

Resolved, That in order to provide proper guaranties for security in the future, so that peace and prosperity shall surely prevail, and the plighted faith of the nation be preserved, it is the first duty of Congress to take care that no State declared in rebellion shall be allowed to resume its relations with the Union until after satisfactory performance of five several conditions, which conditions precedent must be submitted to a popular vote, and be sanctioned by a majority of the people of each State respectively, as follows.

1. The complete reëstablishment of loyalty, as shown by honest recognition of the unity of the Republic, and the duty of allegiance to it at all times, without mental reservation or equivocation of any kind.

2. The complete suppression of all oligarchical pretensions, and the complete enfranchisement of all citizens, so that there shall be no denial of rights on account of race or color, but justice shall be impartial, and all shall be equal before the law.

†From: Charles Sumner, *The Works of Charles Sumner,* 12 vols. (Boston, 1874), vol. 10, pp. 33-34.

3. The rejection of the Rebel debt, and at the same time the adoption, in just proportion, of the national debt and the national obligations to Union soldiers, with solemn pledges never to join in any measure, direct or indirect, for their repudiation, or in any way tending to impair the national credit.

4. The organization of an educational system for the equal benefit of all, without distinction of race or color.

5. The choice of citizens for office, whether State or National, of constant and undoubted loyalty, whose conduct and conservation shall give assurance of peace and reconciliation.

Resolved, That to provide these essential safeguards, without which the national security and the national faith will be imperilled, States cannot be precipitated back to political power and independence; but they must wait until these conditions are in all respects fulfilled.

Document 5-b†

Thaddeus Stevens on Territorialization and Confiscation

[Stevens, informally recognized as what we would now call the majority leader in the House of Representatives, made the following comments in major speeches delivered in the House in 1865 and 1866. He recognized that most of his Republican colleagues did not share his position, however, and soothed them by adding, "I trust the Republican party will not be alarmed at what I am saying. I do not profess to speak their sentiments, nor must they be held responsible for them."]

It is obvious from all this that the first duty of Congress is to pass a law declaring the condition of these outside or defunct States, and providing proper civil governments for them. Since the conquest they have been governed by martial law. Military rule is necessarily despotic, and ought not to exist longer than is absolutely necessary. As there are no symptoms that the people of these provinces will be prepared to participate in constitutional government for some years, I know of no arrangement so proper for them as territorial governments. There they can learn the principles of freedom and eat the fruit of foul rebellion. Under such governments, while electing members to the Territorial Legislatures, they will necessarily mingle with those to whom Congress shall extend the right of suffrage. In territories Congress fixed the qualifications of electors; and I know of no better place nor better occasions for the conquered rebels and the conqueror to practice justice to all men, and to accustom themselves to make and to obey equal laws. . . .

But this is not all that we ought to do before these inveterate rebels are invited to participate in our legislation. We have turned, or are about to turn, loose four million slaves without a hut to shelter them or a cent in their

†From: U.S., Congress, *Congressional Globe,* 39th cong., 1st sess., December 18, 1865, p. 74.

pockets. The infernal laws of slavery have prevented them from acquiring an education, understanding the commonest laws of contract, or of managing the ordinary business of life. This Congress is bound to provide for them until they can take care of themselves. If we do not furnish them with homesteads from forfeited rebel property, and hedge them around with protective laws; if we leave them to the legislation of their late masters, we had better left them in bondage. Their condition would be worse than that of our prisoners at Andersonville, If we fail in this great duty now, when we have the power, we shall deserve and receive the execration of history and of all future ages.

Document 5-c†

George W. Julian's Program of Reconstruction

[Julian was one of the most radical of the Republican congressmen, on occasion breaking even with Stevens. He delivered this speech before the Indiana state legislature on November 17, 1865 and called it "Dangers and Duties of the Hour—Reconstruction and Suffrage."]

I would hang liberally . . . . I would make the gallows respectable in these latter days, by dedicating it to Christian uses. I would dispose of a score or two of the most conspicuous of the rebel leaders, not for vengeance, but to satisfy public justice, and make expensive the enterprise of treason for all time to come. . . . If these men are not punished, and you allow the infernal poison to sift itself down into the general mind that treason is no crime, in a little while we shall be shaking hands with our dear Southern brethren, the government may get back into its old ruts, and another horrid war may be the harvest of our recreancy to our trust.

But suppose you were to hang or exile all these leaders, . . . your work, then, is only just begun. You ought, in the next place, to take their large landed estates and parcel them out among our soldiers and seamen, and the poor people of the South, black and white, as a basis of real democracy and genuine civilization. . . . The leading rebels in the South are the great landlords of that country. One half to three fourths of all the cultivated land belongs to them, and if you would take it, as you have the right to do, by confiscation, you would not disturb the rights of the great body of the people in the South, for they never owned the land. . . . If you don't do something of that kind, you will have in the rebel States a system of serfdom over the poor almost as much to be deplored as slavery itself. Rich Yankees will go down there . . . and buy up these estates and establish a system of wages-slavery, of serfdom over the poor, that would be just as intolerable as the old system of servitude. . . .

You want no order of nobility there save that of the laboring masses. Instead of large estates, widely scattered settlements, wasteful agriculture,

†From: George W. Julian, *Speeches on Political Questions* (New York and Cambridge, Mass., 1872), pp. 262-90.

popular ignorance, social degradation, the decline of manufactures, contempt for honest labor, and a pampered oligarchy, you want small farms, thrifty tillage, free schools, social independence, flourishing manufactures and the arts, respect for honest labor, and equality of political rights. You can lay hold of these blessings, on the one hand, or these corresponding curses, on the other, just as you please. Those regions are in your plastic hands. . . .

But suppose you have hung or exiled the leaders of the rebellion, and disposed of their great landed estates in the way indicated; your work is then only half done. Without something else, you will fail after all to reap the full rewards of your sufferings and sacrifices. In order to complete your work of reconstruction, you must put the ballot into the hands of the loyal men of the South. . . .

I would have Congress put a territorial government over her [each southern state], and President Johnson to appoint a chief justice, a governor, a marshal, etc., and in local politics, in electing justices, constables, etc., I would set the people to voting. If I should allow the rebels to vote, I would be sure to checkmate them by the votes of loyal negroes; and thus I would train up the people, black and white, to the use of the ballot. If they should go astray, the supervisory power of Congress would correct all mistakes; and after a while, when a population had been secured fit for State government, I would, if in Congress, vote to receive Carolina again into our embrace. Some of the States might be received sooner, and under less exacting conditions than others; but in all, I would want to be assured that no future harm to our peace could result from any lack of vigilance on our part in prescribing necessary conditions.

6

Nonradical Republicans on Reconstruction 1865-1866

Conservative and moderate Republicans reached a pretty general consensus regarding the minimum terms of Reconstruction upon which they would insist. Those terms did not include the imposition of black suffrage, although many moderates favored it if limited by educational restrictions.

Document 6-a†

Schuyler Colfax

[Colfax was the Speaker of the House of Representatives and delivered the speech from which the following passages are excerpted upon his arrival in Washington, November 18, 1865 in response to a serenade by political supporters. He intended it to be a clear statement of the position of the moderate congressional leadership, a notice to President Johnson that the leaders desired no extreme measures but that they would not acquiesce in his policy without some additions.]

It is auspicious that the ablest Congress that has sat during my knowledge in public affairs meets next month, to face and settle the momentous questions which will be brought before it. It will not be governed by any spirit of revenge, but solely by duty to the country. I have no right to anticipate its action, nor do I bind myself to any inflexible, unalterable policy. But these ideas occur to me, and I speak of them with the frankness with which we should always express our views. . . . Some of those members of the so-called Confederate Congress, who at our adjournment last March, were struggling to blot this nation from the map of the world, propose, I understand, to enter Congress on the opening day of the session next month and resume their former business of governing the country they struggled so earnestly to ruin. They say they have lost no rights. . . . The constitution, which seems framed for every emergency, gives to each house the exclusive right to judge of the qualifications of the election returns of its members, and I apprehend they will exercise that right. Congress having passed no law on reconstruction, President Johnson prescribed certain action for these States

†From: *New York Times*, November 19, 1865.

which he deemed indispensable to their restoration to their former relations to the government, which I think eminently wise and patriotic. . . . But there are other terms on which, I think, there is no division among the loyal men of the Union. First, that the Declaration of Independence must be recognized as the law of the land, and every man, alien and native, white and black, protected in the inalienable and God-given rights of "life, liberty and the pursuit of happiness." Mr. Lincoln in that Emancipation Proclamation, which is the proudest wreath in his chaplet of fame, not only gave freedom to the slave, but declared that the government would maintain that freedom. We cannot abandon them and leave them defenceless at the mercy of their former owners. They must be protected in their rights of person and property, and these freemen must have the right to sue in courts of justice for all just claims, and to testify also, so as to have security against outrage and wrong. . . . Second—The amendments of their State constitutions which have been adopted by many of their state conventions so reluctantly, under the pressure of dispatches from the President and the Secretary of State, should be ratified by a majority of the people. . . . Third—The President can on all occasions insist that they should elect Congressmen who could take the [ironclad test] oath prescribed by the Act of 1862. . . . Fourth—While it must be expected that a minority of these States will cherish for years, perhaps, their feelings of disloyalty, the country has a right to expect that before their members are admitted to a share in the government of this country a clear majority of the people of each of these States should give evidence of their earnest and cheerful loyalty. . . . The danger now is in too much precipitation. Let us rather make haste slowly, and we can then hope that the foundations of our government, when thus reconstructed on the basis of indisputable loyalty will be as eternal as the stars.

Document 6-b†

Henry C. Deming

[Deming, a Republican representative from Connecticut, was among the most conservative members of his party in Congress. Still, note his hint at black suffrage. He offered his suggestions in the House on January 19, 1866.]

I am now prepared to declare with precision, but with brevity, what the national security and the public faith, in my judgment, require as conditions precedent to the readmission to the public councils of "public enemies" from States who for more than four years have deliberately divested themselves of every legal idea of a State as defined by public law, and of all the elements of a State which the Constitution of the United States enjoins them to possess and maintain.

It requires, first, that the Government shall be absolutely protected from a repetition of the secession experiment by a provision in our organic law;

†From: U.S., Congress, *Congressional Globe*, 39th Cong., 1st sess., p. 331.

second, that the freedman shall be secured an absolute equality with the white man before the civil and criminal law, and shall be endowed with every political right necessary to maintain that equality; third, that the public creditor shall be protected, as completely as organic law can protect him, from any repudiation or scaling down of the public debt; fourth, that the citizens, both of the rebel and loyal States, shall be protected, as completely as organic law can protect them, from any taxation, direct or indirect, for the payment of the rebel debt; and unless the equality of the freedman before both civil and criminal law can be fortified by legislation here, under the second clause of the amendment to the Constitution, giving universal freedom to the slave, we shall require, fifth, an amendment similar to that introduced by my distinguished friend from Ohio, [Mr. Bingham,]

"That Congress shall have power to make all laws necessary and proper to secure to all persons in every State equal protection in their rights of life, liberty, and property."

Much more than this we might rightfully demand; much more than this we might reasonably claim; but not a jot less can we fail to secure as conditions precedent to the readmission of these "public enemies" to the public councils without being guilty of treachery to the living, to the dead, and to those who are yet to be.

7

Dana's "Grasp of War" Speech

Richard Henry Dana, whose constitutional interpretation of the Civil War was accepted by the Supreme Court in the *Prize Cases* (1863), offered this justification for national power over the South in Reconstruction at a mass meeting in Boston on June 21, 1865. In this speech, Dana articulated what would become the most widely accepted Republican constitutional argument on the subject. Note Data's concern that the traditional balance between the state and national governments be preserved.

Document†
We wish to know, I suppose, first, What are our powers? . . . Second—What ought we to do? Third—How ought we to do it? . . .

. . . We stand upon the ground of war, and we exercise the powers of war.

Now, my fellow citizens, what are those powers and rights? What is a WAR? War is not an attempt to kill, to destroy; but it is *coercion for a purpose.* . . . A war is over when its purpose is secured. It is a fatal mistake to hold that this war is over, because the fighting has ceased. This war is not over. We are in the attitude and in the *status* of war to-day. There is the solution of this question. . . .

When one nation has conquered another, in a war, the victorious nation does not retreat from the country and give up possession of it, because the fighting has ceased. No; it holds the conquered enemy in the grasp of war until it has secured whatever it has a right to acquire. I put that proposition fearlessly—*The conquering party may hold the other in the grasp of war until it has secured whatever it has a right to require.* . . . [Dana then discussed what he believed the nation could and ought to require: full emancipation, including equal civil and political rights.]

This, then, fellow citizens, is what we have a right to demand. Now comes my third question—How do you propose to accomplish it? . . . The right to acquire a homestead, the right to testify in courts, the right to vote, by the Constitution, depend, not only in spirit, but in the letter, upon the state constitutions. . . . What are you going to do about it?

You find the answer in my first proposition. We are in a state of war. We are exercising war powers. We hold each state in the grasp of war until the state does what we have a right to require of her. . . .

The conqueror must choose between two courses—to permit the political institutions, the body politic, to go on, and treat with it, or obliterate it. We

†From: Richard Henry Dana, Jr., *Speeches in Stirring Times and Letters to a Son,* ed. Richard Henry Dana III (Boston and New York: Houghton Mifflin Co., 1910), pp. 243-59.

have destroyed and obliterated their central government. Its existence was treason. As to their states, we mean to adhere to the first course. We mean to say the states shall remain, with new constitutions, new systems. We do not mean to exercise sovereign civil jurisdiction over them in our Congress. . . . Our system is a planetary system; each planet revolving around its orbit, and all round a common sun. This system is held together by a balance of powers—centripetal and centrifugal forces. We have established a wise balance of forces. Let not that balance be destroyed. . . .

Our system is a system of states, with central power; and in that system is our safety. . . . Let the [southern] states make their own constitutions, but the constitutions must be satisfactory to the Republic. . . .

8

Congress's Reconstruction Legislation

Document 8-a†

The Freedmen's Bureau Bill

[The Freedmen's Bureau was created by congressional act in 1865. This bill was designed to extend its life and to broaden its activities. Congress failed to pass it over President's Johnson's veto but passed a similar bill over the veto after his final break with the Republican party.]

Be it enacted, c., That the act to establish a bureau for the relief of freedmen and refugees [in 1865] ... shall continue in force until otherwise provided by law, and shall extend to refugees and freedmen in all parts of the United States....

Sec. 3. That the Secretary of War may direct such issues of provisions, clothing, fuel, and other supplies, including medical stores and transportation ... as he may deem needful for the immediate and temporary shelter and supply of destitute and suffering refugees and freedmen....

Sec. 6. That the commissioner [of the Freedmen's Bureau] shall, under the direction of the President, procure in the name of the United States ... such lands ... as may be required for refugees and freedmen dependent on the Government for support; and he shall provide or cause to be erected suitable buildings for asylums and schools....

Sec. 7. That ... in any [insurrectionary] State ... wherein, in consequences of any State or local law, ordinance, police or other regulation, custom, or prejudice, any of the civil rights or immunites belonging to white persons ... are refused or denied to negroes ... or wherein they ... are subjected to any other or different punishment, pains, or penalties, for the commission of any act or offence than are prescribed for white persons.... it shall be the duty of the President of the United States, through the commissioner, to extend military protection and jurisdiction over all cases affecting such persons so discriminated against.

---

†From: Edward McPherson, ed., *The Political History of the United States During* ... *Reconstruction,* 2d ed. (Washington, D.C., 1875), pp. 72-74.

Document 8-b†

The Civil Rights Bill

All persons born in the United States and not subject to any foreign power, excluding Indians not taxed, are hereby declared to be citizens of the United States; and such citizens, of every race and color, without regard to any previous condition of slavery or involuntary servitude, except as a punishment for crime whereof the party shall have been duly convicted, shall have the same right, in every State and Territory in the United States, to make and enforce contracts, to sue, be parties, and give evidence, to inherit, purchase, lease, sell, hold, and convey real and personal property, and to full and equal benefit of all laws and proceedings for the security of person and property, as is enjoyed by white citizens, and shall be subject to like punishment, pains and penalties, and to none other, any law, statute, ordinance, regulation, or custom, to the contrary notwithstanding.

Sec. 2. .... Any person who, under color of any law, statute, ordinance, regulation, or custom, shall subject, or cause to be subjected, any inhabitant of any State or Territory to the deprivation of any right secured or protected by this act, or to different punishment, pains, or penalties on account of such person having at any time been held in a condition of slavery or involuntary servitude, ... or by reason of his color or race, than is prescribed for the punishment of white persons, shall be deemed guilty of a misdemeanor, and, on conviction, shall be punished by fine not exceeding one thousand dollars, or imprisonment not exceeding one year, or both, in the discretion of the court.

Sec. 3. ... The district courts of the United States ... shall have, exclusively of the courts of the several States, cognizance of all crimes and offenses committed against the provisions of this act, and also, concurrently with the circuit courts of the United States, of all causes, civil and criminal, affecting persons who are denied or cannot enforce in the courts or judicial tribunals of the State or locality where they may be any of the rights secured to them by the first section of this act; and if any suit or prosecution, civil or criminal, has been or shall be commenced in any State court, against any such person, for any cause whatsoever, ... such defendant shall have the right to remove such cause for trial to the proper district or circuit court.

†From: *U.S., Statutes at Large*, vol. 14, pp. 27-29. Note the removal provisions of section 3.

9

Johnson Rejects Congress's Program

Document 9-a†

The Freedmen's Bureau Bill Veto

[President Johnson sent this veto to the Senate on February 19, 1866. Powerful and well written, the veto won a fair amount of support among Republicans, both in Congress and in the nation, and the Senate's attempt to override it failed. Johnson's criticism of military courts struck a responsive chord, but his closing paragraphs, which seemed to preclude any role for Congress in the Reconstruction process, alienated many who otherwise would have sustained him.]

Jurisdiction is to extend . . . over all cases affecting freedmen and refugees discriminated against "by local law, custom, or prejudice." In those eleven States the bill subjects any white person who may be charged with depriving a freedman of "any civil rights or immunities belonging to white persons" to imprisonment or fine, or both. . . . This military jurisdiction also extends to all questions that may arise respecting contracts. The agent who is thus to exercise the office of a military judge may be a stranger, entirely ignorant of the laws of the place, and exposed to the errors of judgment to which all men are liable. The exercise of power over which there is no legal supervision by so vast a number of agents as is contemplated by the bill must, by the very nature of man, be attended by acts of caprice, injustice, and passion.

The trials having their origin under this bill are to take place without the intervention of a jury and without any fixed rules of law or evidence. The rules on which offenses are to be "heard and determined" by the numerous agents are such rules and regulations as the President, through the War Department, shall prescribe. No previous presentment is required nor any indictment charging the commission of a crime against the laws. . . . The punishment will be, not what the law declares, but such as a court-martial may think proper; and from these arbitrary tribunals there lies no appeal, no writ of error to any of the courts in which the Constitution of the United States vests exclusively the judicial power of the country.

I can not reconcile a system of military jurisdiction of this kind with the words of the Constitution which declare that "no person shall be held to

†From: James D. Richardson, comp., *A Compilation of the Messages and Papers of the Presidents* . . . , (New York, 1897), vol. 8, pp. 3597, 3599, 3601-3603.

answer for a capital or otherwise infamous crime unless on a presentment or indictment of a grand jury, except in cases arising in the land or naval forces, or in the militia when in actual service in time of war or public danger," and that "in all criminal prosecutions the accused shall enjoy the right to a speedy and public trial by an impartial jury of the State and district wherein the crime shall have been committed." . . .

The third section of the bill authorizes a general and unlimited grant of support to the destitute and suffering refugees and freedmen, their wives and children. Succeeding sections make provision for the rent or purchase of landed estates for freedmen, and for the erection for their benefit of suitable buildings for asylums and schools, the expenses to be defrayed from the Treasury of the whole people. The Congress of the United States has never heretofore thought itself empowered to establish asylums beyond the limits of the District of Columbia, except for the benefit of our disabled soldiers and sailors. It has never founded schools for any class of our own people, not even for the orphans of those who have fallen in the defense of the Union, but has left the care of education to the much more competent and efficient control of the States, of communities, of private associations, and of individuals. It has never deemed itself authorized to expend the public money for the rent or purchase of homes for the thousands, not to say millions, of the white race who are honestly toiling from day to day for their subsistence. A system for the support of indigent persons in the United States was never contemplated by the authors of the Constitution; nor can any good reason be advanced why, as a permanent establishment, it should be founded for one class or color of our people more than another. . . .

The query presents itself whether the system proposed by the bill will not, when put into complete operation, practically transfer the entire care, support, and control of 4,000,000 emancipated slaves to agents, overseers, or taskmasters, who, appointed at Washington, are to be located in every county and parish throughout the United States containing freedmen and refugees. Such a system would inevitably tend to a concentration of power in the Executive which would enable him, if so disposed, to control the action of this numerous class and use them for the attainment of his own political ends.

I can not but add another very grave objection to this bill. The Constitution imperatively declares, in connection with taxation, that each State *shall* have at least one Representative, and fixes the rule for the number to which, in future times, each State shall be entitled. It also provides that the Senate of the United States *shall* be composed of two Senators from each State, and adds with peculiar force "that no State, without its consent, shall be deprived of its equal suffrage in the Senate." . . . At the time, however, of the consideration and the passing of this bill there was no Senator or Representative in Congress from the eleven States which are to be mainly affected by its provisions. . . . I would not interfere with the unquestionable right of Congress to judge, each House for itself, "of the elections, returns, and qualifications of its own members;" but that authority can not be construed as including the right to shut out in time of peace any State from the representation to which it is entitled by the Constitution. . . .

The President of the United States stands toward the country in a somewhat different attitude from that of any member of Congress. Each member of Congress is chosen from a single district or State; the President is chosen by the people of all the States. As eleven States are not at this time represented in either branch of Congress, it would seem to be his duty on all proper occasions to present their just claims to Congress. . . . I hold it my duty to recommend to you, in the interests of peace and the interests of union, the admission of every State to its share in public legislation when, however insubordinate, insurgent, or rebellious its people may have been, it presents itself, not only in an attitude of loyalty and harmony, but in the persons of representatives whose loyalty can not be questioned under any existing constitutional or legal test. . . .

The bill under consideration refers to certain of the States as though they had not "been fully restored in all their constitutional relations to the United States." If they have not, let us at once act together to secure that desirable end at the earliest possible moment. It is hardly necessary for me to inform Congress that in my own judgment most of those States, so far, at least, as depends upon their own action, have already been fully restored, and are to be deemed as entitled to enjoy their constitutional rights as members of the Union.

Document 9-b†

The Civil Rights Bill Veto

[President Johnson delivered this veto on March 27, 1866. This veto seemed to be based much more on racial prejudice and state rights grounds than the veto of the Freedmen's Bureau bill, and it garnered far less support. The Senate passed the bill over the veto on April 9, 1866.]

By the first section of the bill all persons born in the United States and not subject to any foreign power, excluding Indians not taxed, are declared to be citizens of the United States. This provision comprehends the Chinese of the Pacific States, Indians subject to taxation, the people called gypsies, as well as the entire race designated as blacks. . . . Every individual of these races born in the United States is by the bill made a citizen. . . .

The grave question presents itself whether, when eleven of the thirty-six States are unrepresented in Congress at the present time, it is sound policy to make our entire colored population and all other excepted classes citizens of the United States. Four millions of them have just emerged from slavery into freedom. Can it be reasonably supposed that they possess the requisite qualifications to entitle them to all the privileges and immunities of citizens

†From: Ibid., pp. 3601-11.

of the United States? Have the people of the several States expressed such a conviction? . . . The policy of the Government from its origin to the present time seems to have been that persons who are strangers to and unfamiliar with our institutions and our laws should pass through a certain probation, at the end of which, before attaining the coveted prize, they must give evidence of their fitness to receive and to exercise the rights of citizens as contemplated by the Constitution of the United States. The bill in effect proposes a discrimination against large numbers of intelligent, worthy, and patriotic foreigners, and in favor of the negro. . . .

A perfect equality of the white and colored races is attempted to be fixed by Federal law in every State of the Union over the vast field of State jurisdiction covered by these enumerated rights. In no one of these can any State ever exercise any power of discrimination between the different races. In the exercise of State policy over matters exclusively affecting the people of each State it has frequently been thought expedient to discriminate between the two races. By the statutes of some of the States, Northern as well as Southern, it is enacted, for instance, that no white person shall intermarry with a negro or mulatto. . . .

I do not say that this bill repeals State laws on the subject of marriage between the two races. . . . I cite this discrimination, however, as an instance of the State policy as to discrimination, and to inquire whether if Congress can abrogate all State laws of discrimination between the two races in the matter of real estate, of suits, and of contracts generally Congress may not also repeal the State laws as to the contract of marriage between the two races. Hitherto every subject embraced in the enumeration of rights contained in this bill has been considered as exclusively belonging to the States. They all relate to the internal police and economy of the respective States. They are matters which in each State concern the domestic condition of its people, varying in each according to its own peculiar circumstances and the safety and well-being of its own citizens. . . .

If, in any State which denies to a colored person any one of all those rights, that person should commit a crime against the laws of a State—murder, arson, rape, or any other crime—all protection and punishment through the courts of the State are taken away, and he can only be tried and punished in the Federal courts. . . . So that over this vast domain of criminal jurisprudence provided by each State for the protection of its own citizens and for the punishment of all persons who violate its criminal laws, Federal law, whenever it can be made to apply, displaces State law. . . . This section of the bill undoubtedly comprehends cases and authorizes the exercise of powers that are not, by the Constitution, within the jurisdiction of the courts of the United States. . . .

I do not propose to consider the policy of this bill. To me the details of the bill seem fraught with evil. The white race and the black race of the South have hitherto lived together under the relation of master and slave—capital owning labor. Now, suddenly, that relation is changed, and as to ownership capital and labor are divorced. They stand now each master of itself. In this new relation, one being necessary to the other, there will be a new adjustment, which both are deeply interested in making harmonious. . . .

This bill frustrates this adjustment. It intervenes between capital and labor and attempts to settle questions of political economy through the agency of numerous officials whose interest it will be to foment discord between the two races, for as the breach widens their employment will continue, and when it is closed their occupation will terminate.

In all our history, in all our experience as a people living under Federal and State law, no such system as that contemplated by the details of this bill has ever before been proposed or adopted. They establish for the security of the colored race safeguards which go infinitely beyond any that the General Government has ever provided for the white race. In fact, the distinction of race and color is by the bill made to operate in favor of the colored and against the white race. They interfere with the municipal legislation of the States, with the relations existing exclusively between a State and its citizens, or between inhabitants of the same State—an absorption and assumption of power by the General Government which, if acquiesced in, must sap and destroy our federative system of limited powers and break down the barriers which preserve the rights of the States. It is another step, or rather stride, toward centralization and the concentration of all legislative powers in the National Government. The tendency of the bill must be to resuscitate the spirit of rebellion and to arrest the progress of those influences which are more closely drawing around the States the bonds of union and peace.

10

The First Congressional Reconstruction Program

Document 10-a†

Report of the Reconstruction Committee

[The Joint Committee of Fifteen on Reconstruction reported its proposals to both houses of Congress on April 30, 1866. They suggested an amendment to the Constitution and two bills. One of them disqualified Confederate leaders from national office, and the other, reprinted below, defined exactly how the insurrectionary states could be restored to normal relations in the Union. Note that the report followed the logic of Dana's "Grasp of War" speech and shared his concern that the war's constitutional dislocations be ended as quickly as possible.]

A claim for the immediate admission of senators and representatives from the so-called Confederate States has been urged, which seems to your committee not to be founded either in reason or in law, and which cannot be passed without comment. Stated in a few words, it amounts to this: That inasmuch as the lately insurgent States had no legal right to separate themselves from the Union, they still retain their positions as States, and consequently the people thereof have a right to immediate representation in Congress without the imposition of any conditions whatever; and further, that until such admission Congress has no right to tax them for the support of the government. It has ever been contended that until such admission all legislation affecting their interests is, if not unconstitutional, at least unjustifiable and oppressive.

It is believed by your committee that all these propositions are not only wholly untenable, but, if admitted, would tend to the destruction of the government. . . .

It cannot, we think, be denied by any one, having a tolerable acquaintance with public law, that the war . . . was a civil war of the greatest magnitude. The people waging it were necessarily subject to all the rules which, by the law of nations, control a contest of that character, and to all the legitimate consequences following it. One of those consequences was that, within the

†From: U.S., Congress, *Report of the Joint Committee on Reconstruction* (Washington, D.C., 1866), pp. x-xi, xii-xiii.

limits prescribed by humanity, the conquered rebels were at the mercy of the conquerors. That a government thus outraged had a most perfect right to exact indemnity for the injuries done, and security against the recurrence of such outrages in the future, would seem too clear for dispute. What the nature of that security should be, what proof should be required of a return to allegiance, what time should elapse before a people thus demoralized should be restored in full to the enjoyment of political rights and privileges, are questions for the law-making power to decide, and that decision must depend on grave considerations of the public safety and the general welfare. . . .

We freely admit that such a condition of things should be brought, if possible, to a speedy termination. It is most desirable that the Union of all the States should become perfect at the earliest moment consistent with the peace and welfare of the nation; that all these States should become fully represented in the national councils, and take their share in the legislation of the country. The possession and exercise of more than its just share of power by any section is injurious, as well to that section as to all the others. Its tendency is degrading and demoralizing, and such a state of affairs is only to be tolerated on the ground of a necessary regard to the public safety. As soon as that safety is secured it should terminate.

Document 10-b†

The Fourteenth Amendment

Sec. 1. All persons born or naturalized in the United States, and subject to the jurisdiction thereof, are citizens of the United States and of the State wherein they reside. No State shall make or enforce any law which shall abridge the privileges or immunities of citizens of the United States; nor shall any State deprive any person of life, liberty or property, without due process of law, nor deny to any person within its jurisdiction the equal protection of the laws.

Sec. 2. Representatives shall be apportioned among the several States according to their respective numbers, counting the whole number of persons in each State, excluding Indians not taxed. But when the right to vote at any election for the choice of electors for President and Vice President of the United States, representatives in Congress, the executive and judicial officers of a State, or the members of the Legislature thereof, is denied to any of the male inhabitants of such State, being twenty-one years of age, and citizens of the United States, or in any way abridged, except for participation in rebellion or other crime, the basis of representation therein shall be reduced in the proportion which the number of such male citizens shall bear to the whole number of male citizens twenty-one years of age in said State.

Sec. 3. No Person shall be Senator or Representative in Congress, or elector of President or Vice President, or hold any office, civil or military, under the United States, or under any State, who, having previously taken an

†From: U.S., *Statutes at Large*, vol. 14, pp. 358-59.

oath as a member of Congress, or as an officer of the United States, or as a member of any State Legislature, or as an executive or judicial officer of any State, to support the Constitution of the United States, shall have engaged in insurrection or rebellion against the same, or given aid or comfort to the enemies thereof. But Congress may, by a vote of two-thirds of each House, remove such disability.

Sec. 4. The validity of the public debt of the United States, authorized by law, including debts incurred for payment of pensions and bounties for services in suppressing insurrection or rebellion, shall not be questioned. But neither the United States nor any State shall assume or pay any debt or obligation incurred in aid of insurrection or rebellion against the United States or any claim for the loss or emancipation of any slave; but all such debts, obligations, and claims shall be held illegal and void.

Sec. 5. The Congress shall have power to enforce, by appropriate legislation, the provisions of this article.

Document 10-c†

The Proposed Reconstruction Bill

[This bill would have made the moderate Reconstruction program of 1866 explicit, guaranteeing restoration to normal relations upon ratification of the Fourteenth Amendment. Radical opposition prevented its passage, but most Republicans felt bound to honor its provisions anyway.]

Whereas it is expedient that the States lately in insurrection should, at the earliest day consistent with the future peace and safety of the Union, be restored to full participation in all political rights; and whereas the Congress did, by joint resolution, propose for ratification to the legislatures of the several States . . . an amendment to the Constitution of the United States . . .

Now, therefore—

Be it enacted by the Senate and House of Representatives . . . in Congress assembled, That whenever the . . . amendment shall have become part of the Constitution . . . . and any State lately in insurrection shall have ratified the same, and shall have modified its constitution and laws in conformity therewith, the senators and representatives from such State, if found duly elected and qualified, may . . . be admitted into Congress as such.

†From: U.S., Congress, *Report of the Joint Committee on Reconstruction*, p. v.

11

The Second Congressional Reconstruction Program

Document 11-a†

The Reconstruction Act

[Section 5 is the "Blaine amendment"; its disfranchisement provision and section 6 were added as the price for radical support.]

WHEREAS no legal State governments or adequate protection for life or property now exists in the rebel States of Virginia, North Carolina, South Carolina, Georgia, Mississippi, Alabama, Louisiana, Florida, Texas, and Arkansas; and whereas it is necessary that peace and good order should be enforced in said States until loyalty and republican State governments can be legally established: Therefore

Be it enacted, ... That said rebel States shall be divided into military districts and made subject to the military authority of the United States ...

Sec. 2. ... It shall be the duty of the President to assign to the command of each of said districts an officer of the army, not below the rank of brigadier general, and to detail a sufficient military force to enable such officer to perform his duties and enforce his authority within the district to which he is assigned.

Sec. 3. ... It shall be the duty of each officer assigned as aforesaid to protect all persons in their rights of person and property, to suppress insurrection, disorder, and violence, and to punish, or cause to be punished, all disturbers of the public peace and criminals, and to this end he may allow local civil tribunals to take jurisdiction of and to try offenders, or, when in his judgment it may be necessary for the trial of offenders, he shall have power to organize military commissions or tribunals for that purpose; and all interference under color of State authority with the exercise of military authority under this act shall be null and void. ...

Sec. 5. ... When the people of any one of said rebel States shall have formed a constitution of government in conformity with the Constitution of the United States in all respects, framed by a convention of delegates elected by the male citizens of said State twenty-one years old and upward, of whatever race, color, or previous condition, ... and when such constitution

†From: U.S., *Statutes at Large*, vol. 14, pp. 428-29.

shall provide that the elective franchise shall be enjoyed by all such persons as have the qualifications herein stated for electors of delegates, and when such constitution shall be ratified by a majority of the persons voting on the question of ratification who are qualified as electors of delegates, and when such constitution shall have been submitted to Congress for examination and approval, and Congress shall have approved the same, and when said State, by a vote of its legislature elected under said constitution, shall have adopted the amendment to the Constitution of the United States, proposed by the thirty-ninth Congress, and known as article fourteen, and when said article shall have become a part of the Constitution of the United States, said State shall be declared entitled to representation in Congress, and senators and representatives shall be admitted therefrom on their taking oaths prescribed by law, and then and thereafter the preceding sections of this act shall be inoperative in said State: *Provided*, That no person excluded from the privilege of holding office by said proposed amendment to the Constitution of the United States shall be eligible to election as a member of the convention to frame a constitution for any of said rebel States, nor shall any such person vote for members of such convention.

Sec. 6. . . . Until the people of said rebel States shall be by law admitted to representation in the Congress of the United States, any civil governments which may exist therein shall be deemed provisional only, and in all respects subject to the paramount authority of the United States at any time to abolish, modify or control, or supersede the same; and in all elections to any office under such provisional governments all persons shall be entitled to vote, and none others, who are entitled to vote under the provisions of the fifth section of this act; and no person shall be eligible to any office under any such provisional governments who would be disqualified from holding office under the provisions of the third article of said constitutional amendment.

Document 11-b†

Julian on the Reconstruction Act

[George W. Julian, one of the most radical Republicans in the House, like many radicals demanded long-term territorialization. He opposed the Reconstruction Act when first proposed, but like other radicals, was finally forced to acquiesce in the compromise version.]

I . . . object to the measure before us, that it is a mere enabling act, looking to the early restoration of the rebellious districts to their former places in the Union, instead of a well-considered frame of government, contemplating such restoration at some indefinite future time, and designed to fit them to receive it. They are not ready for reconstruction as

†From: U.S., Congress, *Congressional Globe*, 39th Cong., 2d sess., January 28, 1867, Appendix, pp. 78-79.

independent States on any terms or conditions which Congress might impose; and I believe the time has come for us to say so. ... I think I am safe in saying that if these districts were to-day admitted as States, with the precise political and social elements which we know to exist in them, even with their rebel population disfranchised and the ballot placed in the hands of radical Union men only, irrespective of color, the experiment would be ruinous to the best interests of their loyal people and calamitous to the nation. The withdrawal of Federal intervention and the unchecked operation of local supremacy would as fatally hedge up the way of justice and equality as the rebel ascendancy which now prevails. Why? Simply because no theory of government, no forms of administration, can be trusted, unless adequately supported by public opinion. The power of the great landed aristocracy in these regions, if unrestrained by power from without, would inevitably assert itself. Its political chemistry, obeying its own laws, would very soon crystalize itself into the same forms of treason and lawlessness which to-day hold their undisturbed empire over the existing loyal element. What these regions need, above all things, is not an easy and quick return to their forfeited rights in the Union, but *government*, the strong arm of power, outstretched from the central authority here in Washington, making it safe for the freedmen of the South, safe for her loyal white men, safe for emigrants from the Old World and from the northern States to go and dwell there; safe for northern capital and labor, northern energy and enterprise, and northern ideas to set up their habitation in peace, and thus found a Christian civilization and a living democracy amid the ruins of the past. That, sir, is what the country demands and the rebel power needs. To talk about suddenly building up independent States where the material for such structures is fatally wanting is nonsense. States must *grow*, and to that end their growth must be fostered and protected. The political and social regeneration of the country made desolate by treason is the prime necessity of the hour, and is preliminary to any reconstruction of States. Years of careful pupilage under the authority of the nation may be found necessary, and Congress alone must decide when and upon what conditions the tie rudely broken by treason shall be restored.

Document 11-c†

A "Carpetbagger" Looks at the Reconstruction Acts

[In the late 1870s Albion W. Tourgée, who had emigrated from Ohio to North Carolina in 1865 and had become an active Republican there, published a fictionalized account of his Reconstruction experiences as a state judge. He gave a southern Republican's assessment of the final congressional Reconstruction program.]

---

†From: Tourgée, *A Fools Errand, By One of the Fools* ... (New York, 1880), pp. 125-26.

It must have been well understood by the wise men who devised this short-sighted plan ... that they were giving the power of the re-organized, subordinate republics, into the hands of a race unskilled in public affairs, poor to a degree hardly to be matched in the civilized world, and so ignorant that not five out of a hundred of its voters could read their own ballots, joined with such Adullamites among the native whites as might be willing to face a proscription which would shut the house of God in the face of their families, together with the few men of Northern birth, resident in that section since the close of the war ... who might elect to become permanent citizens, and join in the movement.

Against them was to be pitted the wealth, the intelligence, the organizing skill, the pride, and the hate of a people whom it had taken four years to conquer in open fight when their enemies outnumbered them three to one, who were animated chiefly by the apprehension of what seemed now about to be forced upon them by this miscalled measure of "Reconstruction;" to wit, the equality of the negro race. . . .

Not content with this, they went farther, and, by erecting the rebellious territory into self-regulating and sovereign States, they abandoned these parties like cocks in a pit, to fight out the question of predominance without the possibility of national interference. They said to the colored man, in the language of one of the pseudo-philosophers of that day, "Root, hog, or die!"

It was cheap patriotism, cheap philanthropy, cheap success!

12 ——— The Fifteenth Amendment

Note that this constitutional amendment, like the Fourteenth Amendment, did not give the national government original jurisdiction over citizens' rights—this time the right to vote. It merely prohibited the states from making a racial discrimination.

Document†

Sec. 1. The right of the citizens of the United States to vote shall not be denied or abridged by the United States or by any State on account of race, color, or previous condition of servitude.

Sec. 2. The Congress shall have the power to enforce this article by appropriate legislation.

†From: U.S., *Statutes at Large*, vol. 16, p. 1131.

13

Carpetbaggers and Scalawags

In the opinion of most white southerners the Republican party in the South was a party of "carpetbaggers" and "scalawags." They repeated this so often that even many northern Republicans accepted it as true. Here a Republican member of the congressional committee investigating the Ku Klux Klan questions an Alabama Democratic politician on the words' true meaning.

Document†

Question. You have used the epithets "carpet-baggers," and "scalawags," repeatedly, during the course of your testimony. I wish you would give us an accurate definition of what a carpet-bagger is and what a scalawag is.

Answer. Well, sir, the term carpet-bagger is not applied to northern men who come here to settle in the South, but a carpet-bagger is generally understood to be a man who comes here for office sake, of an ignorant or bad character, and who seeks to array the negroes against the whites; who is a kind of political dry-nurse for the negro population, in order to get office through him.

Question. Then it does not necessarily suppose that he should be a northern man?

Answer. Yes, sir; it does suppose that he is to be a northern man, but it does not apply to all northern men that come here.

Question. If he is an intelligent, educated man, and comes here for office, then he is not a carpet-bagger, I understand?

Answer. No, sir; we do not generally call them carpet-baggers.

Question. If he is a northern man possessed of good character and seeks office he is not a carpet-bagger?

An .... Mr. Chairman, there are so few northern men who come here of intelligence and character, that join the republican party and look for office alone to the negroes, that we have never made a class for them. I have never heard them classified. They stand *sui generis.* I do not know that they have any classification. But the term "carpet-bagger" was applied to the office-seeker from the North who comes here seeking office by the negroes, by arraying their political passions and prejudices against the white people of the community.

Question. The man in addition to that, under your definition, must be an ignorant man and of bad character?

†From: U.S., Congress, *Testimony taken by the Joint Select Committee to Inquire into the Condition of Affairs in the Late Insurrectionary States: Alabama* (Washington, D.C., 1872), vol. 2, pp. 887-88, 891.

Answer: Yes, sir; he is generally of that description. We regard any man as a man of bad character who seeks to create hostility between the races.

Question. Do you regard any republican as a bad character who seeks to obtain the suffrages of the negro population?

Answer. We regard any republican or any man as a man of bad character, whether he is native or foreign born, who seeks to obtain office from the negroes by exciting their passions and prejudices against the whites. We think that a very great evil—very great. We are very intimately associated with the negro race; we have a large number in the country, and we think it essential that we shall live in peace together. . . .

Question. Having given a definition of the carpet-bagger, you may now define scalawag.

Answer. A scalawag is his subservient tool and accomplice, who is a native of the country.

Question. How many of the white race in the county of Madison vote the republican ticket?

Answer. I do not think, and I have very accurate means of judging, that a hundred ever voted it.

Question. You class them all as carpet-baggers and scalawags?

Answer. Yes, sir.

Question. Are all of them seeking office?

Answer. No sir.

Question. Are all of them ignorant men and of bad character?

Answer. No sir. . . .

Question. How do you classify Captain Day, who is clerk, I believe, of the district court of the United States, and *ex officio* commissioner?

Answer. He has never been politically classed. He never took any part in politics at all.

Question. Does he hold office under the Federal Government?

Answer. Yes, sir.

Question. Do you regard him as a carpet-bagger?

Answer. No, sir.

Question. A northern man?

Answer. Yes, sir. . . .

Question. What distinguishes him from the genuine carpet-bagger?

Answer. Because he does not associate with the negroes; he does not seek their society, politically or socially; he has nothing to do with them any more than any other white gentleman in the community.

Question. He votes with the democratic party? . . .

Answer. I think he did. . . .

Question. As I want to get at the true definition of these terms, I will inquire of you if a northern man comes into Alabama intent upon obtaining office, and seeks to obtain an office through the instrumentality of the democratic organization, is he a carpet-bagger?

Answer. No, sir; the term is never applied to a democrat under any circumstances. Figures sometimes calls Judge Dox a democratic carpet-bagger, but that is a misnomer. No democrat who seeks office through the virtue, intelligence, and property of the country, who says, "Gentlemen, your best men are disfranchised by the act of Congress; I do not care particularly about office, but as you cannot hold it I will go there, knock your chains off, and get you a chance."

14 ═══════════════

══════════ Southerners on
Black Suffrage

This petition was sent to Congress by white Alabama Conservatives in January 1868, protesting the imposition of black suffrage.

Document†

It is well known by all who have knowledge on the subject, that while the negroes of the South may be more intelligent and of better morals than those of the same race in any other part of the world where they exist in equal density, yet they are in the main, ignorant generally, wholly unacquainted with the principles of free Governments, improvident, disinclined to work, credulous yet suspicious, dishonest, untruthful, incapable of self-restraint, and easily impelled by want or incited by false and specious counsels, into folly and crime. Exceptions, of course, there are; chiefly among those who have been reared as servants in our domestic circles, and in our cities. But the general character of our colored population is such as we have described. . . .

Are these the people in whom should be vested the high governmental functions of establishing institutions and enacting and enforcing laws to prevent crime, protect property, preserve peace and order in society, and promote industry, enterprise and civilization in Alabama, and the power and honor of the United States? Without property, without industry, without any regard for reputation, without control over their own caprices and strong passions, and without fear of punishment under laws, by courts and through juries which are created by and composed of themselves, or of those whom they elect, how can it be otherwise than that they will bring, to the great injury of themselves as well as of us and our children, blight, crime, ruin and barbarism on this fair land? . . .

Continue over us, if you will do so, your own rule by the sword. Send down among us, honorable and upright men of your own people, of the race to which you and we belong: and ungracious, contrary to wise policy and the institutions of the country, and tyrannous as it will be, no hand will be raised among us to resist by force their authority. But do not, we implore you, abdicate your own rule over us, by transferring us to the blighting, brutalizing and unnatural dominion of an alien and inferior race: a race which has never shown sufficient administrative capacity for the good government of even the tribes into which it has always been broken up in its native seats; and which in all ages, has itself furnished slaves for all the other races of the earth.

---

†From: U.S., Congress, House, 40th Cong., Record Group 233, "Petitions and Memorials" National Archives, Washington, D.C.

15

The Ku
Klux Klan

Document 15-a†

General John B. Gordon on the Loyal Leagues
and the Origin of the Ku Klux Klan

[General Gordon, later Democratic Senator from Georgia, told the congressional committee investigating the Ku Klux Klan that the organization's sole purpose was to protect southern whites from the Republican Union, or Loyal, Leagues, although they had been disbanded in most areas of the South by 1870.]

The instinct of self-protection prompted that organization; the sense of insecurity and danger, particularly in those neighborhoods where the negro population largely predominated. The reasons which led to this organization were three or four. The first and main reason was the organization of the Union League, as they called it, about which we knew nothing more than this: that the negroes would desert the plantations, and go off at night in large numbers; and on being asked where they had been, would reply, sometimes, "We have been to the muster;" sometimes, "We have been to the lodge;" sometimes, "We have been to the meeting." These things were observed for a great length of time. We knew that the "carpet-baggers," as the people of Georgia called these men who came from a distance and had no interest at all with us; who were unknown to us entirely; who from all we could learn about them did not have any very exalted position at their homes—these men were organizing the colored people. We knew that beyond all question. We knew of certain instances where great crime had been committed; where overseers had been driven from plantations, and the negroes had asserted their right to hold the property for their own benefit. Apprehension took possession of the entire public mind of the State. Men were in many instances afraid to go away from their homes and leave their wives and children for fear of outrage. Rapes were already being committed in the country. There was this general organization of the black race on the one hand, and an entire disorganization of the white race on the other hand. ... It was therefore necessary, in order to protect our families from outrage and preserve our own lives, to have something that we could regard as a brotherhood—a combination of the best men of the country, to act purely in

†From: U.S., Congress, *Testimony taken by the Joint Select Committee to inquire into the Condition of Affairs: Georgia*, vol. 1, p. 308.

self-defense, to repel the attack in case we should be attacked by these people. That was the whole object of this organization.

Document 15-b†

Ben Hill on the Klan

[Many southerners insisted that the outrages attributed to the Ku Klux Klan were really committed by Republicans to stir up northern reaction. Here Benjamin H. Hill, a leading Georgia Conservative testifies before a congressional subcommittee investigating violence in Georgia.]

Question. You have not studied this organization?

Answer. I have only investigated a few cases for the purpose of ascertaining who were the guilty offenders. One reason for investigating the few cases was upon the attempt to reconstruct Georgia some time ago, and these Ku-Klux outrages were made to bear very, very heavily against even Union parties [who opposed returning Georgia to military rule]. I wanted to know if that was the case, and if so, I wanted the people to put down the Ku-Klux. In the second place, I arrived at the conclusion that a great many of these outrages were committed by gentlemen who wanted a reconstruction of the State, and committed those outrages to give an excuse for it. I have always thought that two or three of the most outrageous murders committed in the State were really committed by persons of the same political faith of the parties slain.

Question. And committed for the political effect they would have?

Answer. I think so. And a great many of us who have really wanted to be reconstructed have been between fires.

Question. Will you have the kindness to state to what cases you last referred, where persons were killed by their friends?

Answer. I think Ashburn was killed by his own political friends.

Question. So as to have the benefit of the political capital that could be made out of it?

Answer. I do not think the motive for killing Ashburn was altogether that; I think there was a personal grudge, or jealousy on the part of some of his political friends. And though my mind is not positive, I am inclined to believe that this fellow Adkins was killed expressly for political capital by his own friends. I was positive about that at one time, but I am not so positive about it now.

Question. Killed by his own friends?

Answer. Yes, sir; though I think it likely some of the others were in it also. I may be wrong, but that was the conclusion to which I arrived. . . .

Question. So far as I have observed your papers, (and I have examined them both before I came into the State and since, I mean the democratic papers,) two lines of thought on this subject seem to run along through them;

one is to deny the existence of this organization, and the other is to discountenance with unmeasured abuse every effort to punish such offenses, and even to inquire and ascertain whether in fact they exist. . . . Why is that?

Answer. I am unable to give you a very satisfactory reason. I think myself that the great body of our people are really anxious to put down anything of this sort, the great body of our people of the best class, almost without exception. There are a very few, however, who, as you have stated, have denied unconditionally the existence of such things at all, even in the local and sporadic form I have mentioned, for I do not myself believe that they have existed in any other form. I think they have discountenanced the effort of some people to investigate them, first, because they professed to believe that they did not exist; second, because I think a great many of them have honestly been actuated by a simple desire to pander to what was considered sectional prejudice on this subject. I think we have a class of people in our State, and democrats, too, who are willing to use this occasion, as a great many politicians use all occasions to make themselves popular, by simply pandering to what they consider the sectional prejudices of the hour. I think some have been extreme and ultra in denouncing all pretense of lawlessness, merely for the purpose of making political capital for themselves individually.

Question. Take the case of an honest man, desirous to do justice and to know the truth, who reads nothing but the democratic papers in Georgia, would he believe that there had been any of these outrages and enormities committed from anything he would see in those papers, published as matters of information or for the purpose of denouncing them and rebuking them?

Answer. Heretofore, I believe, that if a man was shut up to the information derived from the democratic press of Georgia, he would have believed that there was no such thing; but I believe now the thing would be different. A great many of our papers are awakening to the fact that there is such a thing as I say, local and temporary in its character. I have believed, myself, for a long time, that there have been these local organizations, and I believe they have been . . . not political in their character. Some few have been political, no doubt; I think that in some cases democrats have availed themselves of the public sentiment for the purpose of exterminating a radical; and I believe some colored people have organized for plunder and robbery. But I believe there have been some cases where men have been made victims by their own political friends for party purposes and ends. I think democrats have been guilty; that plunderers and robbers have been guilty; and I believe that radicals have been guilty for the purpose of making [political] capital.

Document 15-c†

A Republican on the Klan

[Compare this statement by a moderate Georgia Republican to those of the Georgia Democrats Gordon and Hill.]

†From: Ibid., vol. 1, pp. 66-68.

Question. Can you state any particulars you may have heard in reference to the attack on Ware?

Answer. Yes, sir; I can state what I heard. A body of about twenty-five or thirty disguised men went one night and met him upon the road. (I think this was the case of Jourdan Ware.) I am not certain that they went to his house. I believe they met him on the road, somewhere or other, and demanded of him his arms and his watch. I believe he gave up his arms, and they shot him upon his refusal to surrender the watch, and he died a day or two afterward.

Question. Did you ever hear that there was any accusation of his having done anything wrong?

Answer. No, sir; I think not, except I believe I did hear that there was some complaint of his impudence, or something of that sort.

Question. We hear from a great many witnesses about the "impudence" of negroes. What is considered in your section of the country "impudence" on the part of a negro?

Answer. Well, it is considered impudence for a negro not to be polite to a white man—not to pull off his hat and bow and scrape to a white man, as was always done formerly.

Question. Do the white people generally expect or require now that kind of submissive deportment on the part of the negroes that they did while the negroes were slaves?

Answer. I do not think they do as a general thing; a great many do.

Question. Are there many white people who do require it?

Answer. Yes, sir; I think there are a great many who do require it, and are not satisfied unless the negroes do it.

Question. Suppose that a negro man has been working for a white man, and they have some difference or dispute in relation to wages, will your people generally allow a negro man to stand up and assert his rights in the same way and in the same language which they would allow to a white man without objection?

Answer. O, no sir, that is not expected at all.

Question. If the colored man does stand up and assert his rights in language which would be considered pardonable and allowable in a white man, that is considered "impudence" in a negro?

Answer. Yes, sir; gross impudence.

Question. Is that species of "impudence" on the part of the negro considered a sufficient excuse by many of your people for chastising a negro, or "dealing with him?"

Answer. Well, some think so. . . .

Question. In your judgment, from what you have seen and heard, is there something of a political character about this organization?

Answer. I think it is entirely political.

Question. What makes you think so?

Answer. Because the parties who are maltreated by these men are generally republicans. I have never known a democrat to be assaulted. . . .

Question. Give the committee your judgment in relation to the object with which this organization has been gotten up. What do its members intend to attain by it?

Answer. Well, sir, my opinion is that the first object of the institution of the Ku-Klux, or these disguised bands, was to cripple any effect that might be produced by Loyal Leagues. That is my opinion—that this organization was an offset to the Loyal Leagues.

Question. But the Ku-Klux organization kept on increasing after the Loyal Leagues were disbanded?

Answer. Yes, sir.

Question. What, in your opinion, is the object of keeping up the Ku-Klux organization and operating it as they do? What do they intend to produce or effect by it?

Answer. My opinion is, that the purpose was to break down the reconstruction acts; that they were dissatisfied with negro suffrage and the reconstruction measures and everybody that was in favor of them.

Question. Do you think this organization was intended to neutralize the votes of the negroes after suffrage had been extended to them?

Answer. Yes, sir, I think so.

Question. How? By intimidating them?

Answer. Any way. Yes, sir, by intimidation.

Question. Making them afraid to exercise the right of suffrage?

Answer. Yes, sir.

Question. Do you believe that the organization and its operations have, in fact, produced that effect?

Answer. I think they have to some extent.

Question. What is the state of feeling which has been produced among the colored people by this armed, disguised organization, and the acts they have committed?

Answer. Well, in my section of the country, the colored people, generally, are afraid now, and have been for some time, to turn out at an election. They are afraid to say much, or to have anything to do with public affairs. I own a plantation on Coosa River, upon which I have, perhaps, about 40 negroes, and some of them have been pretty badly alarmed, afraid to say much. Some have lain out in the woods, afraid to stay at home.

Document 15-d†

A Ku Klux Klan Murder

[The following letters are from the papers of Governor William W. Holden in the North Carolina State Archives. John G. Lea's recollection of the Stephens murder was deposited at the Archives in 1919, and remained unopened until his death in 1935. The spelling errors in the original letters have not been

†From: Papers of Governor William W. Holden, North Carolina State Archives.

corrected. Republican support came from blacks and poorer whites who had not received the benefits of education under the old regime.]

SAMUEL ALLEN TO HOLDEN, MAY 14, 1870.

On the night of the 9th of the presant month, a band of Armed and disguised men about 15 in number, came to my house about 12 o.c. attempted to brake down my doore, but finding themselves unable to do so, then commenced, shooting into my doore. They commenced to call me by my given name, requesting first & then threatning, if I did not open the doore what they would do which at length I concluded it was best to do which I did do, I asked them what they wanted they then demanded that I should cum out, which I refused to do at which moment I descovered one neare the doore attempting to get hold of me I then steped back to get something to protect myself with. The first thing I sucseded in getting hold of was a hevy saber, as I turned I expected nothing els but for them to be write on me. As I heard a nois behind me, which afterwards proved to be my wife trying to shutting the doore agane, and as I reached the doore again I saw one of the K.K. standing in the doore, with his back against the faceing and shuving the doore open at which moment I rushed upon him and tryed to run the . . . saber through him, which I think I must have cum very nearley doing. So as his left side was turned to me I aimed just aboce his hip, I don't think it went in less than six inches. . . . The rest became very much enraged at having one of there men wonded, and began to prepare to burn the house. I made my escape out the back doore, when they discovered me I was about twenty yards from them. They fired on me and run after me untill they found that they could not catch me. . . . They then told my wife that I wounded one of their men and that they would hang me yet and if we was not all away frome here before the next night that they intended to cum back and hang the last one of us, now Gov I dont prepose to leave if I can see any chance to live, all I want is something to protect myself with. Col. Stephens promises me if you will send him arms that he will organiz a squad in my neighbourhood of D.M. and give me command of them, that we can protect our school which the K.K. are a trying to brake up now the sooner this is don the better for us all, hoping to here frome you soon I am as ever your most obt servt.

J. W. STEPHENS TO HOLDEN, MAY 16, 1870.

Enclosed you will pleas find a letter frome Samuel Allen, Esq. a jintleman, as I presume you know whose integratey for trouth and honesty,—& a true Republican can not be doubted, his onley crime with the opposition is that he is a leading republican in his town ship, and trying to mantain a school on his lot for the col. children in his neighbourhood. . . . Allen has cum to me with information, which he will laye before you, which satesfyes me that he canot cum back, untill you can send troops to protect him, & I am satesfyed that I am no safer than he exsept I am better fortifyed againest there assault, now hoping that you are able to send us the protection & armes. . . .

STATEMENT OF CAPTAIN JOHN G. LEA, JULY 2, 1919 AT THE
REQUEST OF THE NORTH CAROLINA HISTORICAL COMMISSION.

Immediately after the surrender of General Lee, in April, 1865, a bummer named Albion W. Tourgee, of New York, from Sherman's army, came to Caswell County and organized a Union League, and they were drilling every night and beating the drums, and he made many speeches telling the negroes that he was sent by the government and that he would see that they got forty acres of land. He succeeded in getting J. W. Stevens and Jim Jones appointed justices of the peace of Caswell County and they annoyed the farmers very much by holding court every day, persuading the darkies to warrant the farmer, &c. . . .

The first trial that Jim Jones had, a negro stole Captain Mitchell's hog. He was caught cleaning the hog by Mitchell's son and by a darky whose name was Paul McGee. He was carried before Jones and Jones turned him loose and said he had been appointed by Governor Holden to protect the negro and that he intended to do it. Soon thereafter I formed the Ku Klux Klan and was elected county organizer. I organized a den in every township in the county and the Ku Klux whipped Jones and drove him out of the county.

J. W. Stevens burned the hotel in Yanceyville and a row of brick stores. He also burned Gen. William Lee's entire crop of tobacco, and Mr. Sam Hinton's crop. Ed. Slade, a darky, told that he burned the barn of tobacco by an order of Stevens and another darky told about his burning the hotel, also by an order. Stevens was tried by the Ku Klux Klan and sentenced to death. He had a fair trial before a jury of twelve men. At a democratic convention he approached ex-sheriff Wiley and tried to get him to run on the republican ticket for sheriff. Wiley said he would let him know that day. He came to me and informed me of that fact and suggested that he would fool him into that room in which he was killed. . . . A democratic convention was in session in the court room on the second floor of the courthouse in Yanceyville, to nominate county officers and members of the Legislature. . . . I had ordered all the Ku Klux Klan in the county to meet at Yanceyville that day, with their uniforms under their saddles, and they were present. . . . Just before the convention closed, Wiley beckoned to Stevens and carried him down stairs, and Captain Mitchell, James Denny and Joe Fowler went into the room and Wiley came out. Mitchell proceeded to disarm him (he had three pistols on his body). He soon came out and left Jim Denny with a pistol at his head and went to Wiley and told him that he couldn't kill him himself. Wiley came to me and said "You must do something; I am exposed unless you do." Immediately I rushed into the room, with eight or ten men, found him sitting flat on the floor. He arose and approached me and we went and sat down where the wood had been taken away, in an opening in the wood on the wood-pile, and he asked me not to let them kill him. Captain Mitchell rushed at him with a rope, drew it around his neck, put his feet against his chest and by that time about a half dozen men rushed up: Tom Oliver, Pink Morgan, Dr. Richmond and Joe Fowler. Stevens was then stabbed in the breast and also in the neck by Tom. Oliver, and the knife was thrown at his feet and the rope left around his neck. We all came out, closed the door and locked it on the outside and took the key and threw it into County Line Creek.

16

The Ku Klux Klan Act

Document†

Be it enacted ...

Sec. 2. That if two or more persons within any State or Territory of the United States ... shall conspire together, or go in disguise upon the public highway or upon the premises of another for the purpose, either directly or indirectly, of depriving any person or any class of persons of the equal protection of the laws, or of equal privileges or immunities under the laws, or for the purpose of preventing or hindering the constituted authorities of any State from giving or securing to all persons within such State the equal protection of the laws, ... or by force, intimidation, or threat to prevent any citizen of the United States lawfully entitled to vote from giving his support or advocacy in a lawful manner towards or in favor of the election of any lawfully qualified person as an elector of President or Vice-President of the United States, or as a member of the Congress of the United States, or to injure any such citizen in his person or property on account of such support or advocacy, each and every person so offending shall be deemed guilty of a high crime, and, upon conviction thereof in any district or supreme court of any Territory of the United States having jurisdiction of similar offenses shall be punished by a fine not less than five hundred nor more than five thousand dollars, or by imprisonment, with or without hard labor, as the court may determine, for a period of not less than six months nor more than six years, as the court may determine, or by both such fine and imprisonment as the court may determine....

Sec. 3. That in all cases where insurrection, domestic violence, unlawful combinations, or conspiracies in any State shall so obstruct or hinder the execution of the laws thereof, and of the United States, as to deprive any portion or class of the people of such State of any of the rights, privileges, or immunities, or protection, named in the Constitution and secured by this act, and the constituted authorities of such State shall either be unable to protect, or shall from any cause fail in or refuse protection of the people in such rights, such facts will be deemed a denial by such State of the equal protection of the laws to which they are entitled under the Constitution of the United States; and in all such cases, ... it shall be lawful for the President, and it shall be his duty to take such measures, by the employment of the militia or the land and naval forces of the United States, or of either, or by other means, as he

†From: *U.S. Statutes at Large*, vol. 17, pp. 13-15.

131

may deem necessary for the suppression of such insurrection, domestic violence, or combinations. . . .

Sec. 4. That whenever in any State or part of a State the unlawful combinations named in the preceding section of this act shall be organized and armed, and so numerous and powerful as to be able, by violence, to either overthrow or set at defiance the constituted authorities of such State, and of the United States within such State, or when the constituted authorities are in complicity with, or shall connive at the unlawful purposes of, such powerful and armed combinations . . . it shall be lawful for the President of the United States, when in his judgment the public safety shall require it, to suspend the privileges of the writ of habeas corpus, to the end that such rebellion may be overthrown: *Provided,* . . . That the President shall first have made proclamation, as now provided by law, commanding such insurgents to disperse: *And Provided also,* That the provisions of this section shall not be in force after the end of the next regular session of Congress.

17

The Election of 1874 in Alabama

The election of 1874 in Alabama amounted to a "peaceful" revolution according to the pro-Democratic historian Walter L. Fleming. Here Fleming describes the most serious disturbance. His restrained account was based on Democratic sources. Contrast it with the account of Judge Keils himself.

Document†

The evidence is clear that the desperate Radical whites encouraged the blacks to violent conduct in order to cause collisions between the races and thus secure Federal interference. In Eufaula occurred the most serious riot of the Reconstruction period that occurred in Alabama. The negroes came armed and threatening to the polls, which were held by a Republican sheriff and forty Republican deputies. Judge Keils, a carpet-bagger, had advised the blacks to come to Eufaula to vote: "You go to town; there are several troops of Yankees there; these damned Democrats won't shoot a frog. You come armed and do as you please." Order was kept until a negro tried to vote the Democratic ticket and was discovered and mobbed by other blacks. The whites tried to protect him and some negro fired a shot. Then the riot began. The few whites were heavily armed and the negroes also. The deputies, it was said, lost their heads and fired indiscriminately. When the fight was over it was found that ten whites were wounded, and four negroes killed and sixty wounded. The Federal troops came leisurely in after it was over, and surrounded the polls. The course of the Federal troops in Eufaula was much as it was elsewhere. They camped some distance from the polls, and when their aid was demanded by the Republicans the captain either directly refused to interfere, or consulted his orders or his telegrams or his law dictionary. At last he offered to *notify* the white men wanted by the marshal to meet the latter and be arrested. Another commander, who took possession of the polls in Opelika in order to prevent a riot, was censured by General McDowell, the department commander. The troops were weary of such work, and their orders from General McDowell were very vague. After the election, as was to be expected, an outcry arose from the Radicals that the troops had in every case failed to do their duty.

†From: Walter L. Fleming, *Civil War and Reconstruction in Alabama* (New York: Columbia University Press, 1905), pp. 794-95.

E.M. KEILS TO THE EDITORS OF THE MONTGOMERY
ALABAMA STATE JOURNAL

I telegraped you last night that my son Willie was dead. This you must know is almost overwhelming me—I am in poor condition to write. Just at dark, before the counting of votes had commenced at Spring Hill, the crowd rushed into the room, and commenced firing at me. When they entered, I stepped to the end of the counter (the election was held in an old store) pulling Willie behind me to prevent him being shot. Several shots were fired at me, when the lamp was smashed. All was dark then, and Willie and myself stepped behind the counter and sit down under it. A vigorous firing then commenced at the end of the counter, which I thought at the instant were entering the counter and doing no damage. It was at this time Willie was shot, one ball entering the bowels, and the other three entering the right thigh. Willie did not flinch or complain, though his hand was on my shoulder while he was being murdered, so that I knew nothing of it till after those (or the one) who murdered him had moved off. If I had known he was being shot, I could easily have killed the fellow; but as soon as he moved off Willie said to me, "Pa, let us try to get out, I am shot to pieces." This was the first intimation I had that he was shot. Then I told him to be quiet a little longer. But just then several gentlemen rushed to me and assured me they would protect me, and they did. Then I missed Willie's hand from my shoulder, felt for him in the dark, but could not find him. As he (Willie) told me afterwards, some demon seized him by the leg, dragged him on the floor, and kicked him. There was such firing and yells that I heard nothing of this brutal dragging and kicking at that time. The mob was yelling "kill him," "shoot him," "d——n him," "kill him," etc. One or two of those who saved me (they were of the better class of Democrats) went to see after Willie, found him, and carried him away, with the assistance of some colored men. I found him at Dr. Davie's near by, to which place I was carried a few minutes after. He, myself, and wife and daughter, who went to Spring Hill at once, as soon as they could get there, were all treated well at Dr. D.'s, and by the neighbors.

This was a put up job to destroy the ballot box, in which there was 450 or 500 Republican majority, and murder me. And their treatment in dragging and kicking Willie, and telling him as they did, "God d——n you get out of here," shows that they were quite willing to kill him, as me, because they *knew* it was not me they were kicking and dragging, although it was dark in the room.

Willie was in his 17th year, and a better, high-toned, more honorable boy, never lived I am sure. He did no one any harm. He said to me often during the canvass, that he knew I was in danger, and wanted to go with me to Republican meetings, and he went with me to most of them. Then he wanted to go with me to Spring Hill to the election, as he did. When some firing was done out in the crowd, and he thought I was in danger inside the room, he said he wanted to come in, the managers consented, and this is why he was in there.

I feel that I can never get over his death. [Montgomery *Alabama State Journal,* November 9, 1874.]

DEMOCRATIC NEWSPAPERS ON THE EUFAULA RIOT

Big riot today. Several killed and many other hurt. Some badly, but none of our friends among them. The white man's goose hangs high. Three cheers for Eufaula. [Montgomery *Morning News,* November 4, 1874.]

The riot today was provoked by a negro drawing a pistol and abusing and attempting to whip a negro for voting the Democratic ticket. [*Montgomery Advertiser,* November 4, 1874.]

18

Presidential Intervention in a Southern State

When Joseph Brooks, the Liberal Republican-Democratic candidate for governor of Arkansas in 1872, won a court case declaring him rather than Elisha Baxter governor of Arkansas, it presented a thorny problem to President Grant and Attorney General George H. Williams. Baxter had been declared governor by the state legislature, which had counted the election returns as the state constitution required. Brooks claimed that the court judgment entitled him to the place nonetheless. His claim was sustained by a state supreme court judgment affirming the competence of the original court to hear the case. At first the two claimants agreed to Grant's compromise, providing that both of them would call the state legislature into session on May 25 and let it decide the question. But then Grant acceded to Baxter's suggestion that the question be submitted to a legislature called by him alone. Brooks, suspecting treachery, claimed that this was not the proposition to which he had agreed and asked Grant to decide the matter himself. This Grant did on the advice of Williams. It should be noted that through the vagaries of politics by 1874—when this crisis arose—Brooks was supported by most of the Republicans of Arkansas and Baxter by most of the Democrats.

Document†
I have been advised by public rumor that in the State circuit court for this county, in a long pending case brought by Jos. Brooks for the office of Governor of this State, a demurrer to the complainant was overruled, and immediately judgment of ouster against me given. This was done in the absense of counsel for me, and without notice, and immediately thereafter the circuit judge adjourned his court. The claimant has taken possession of the State buildings and ejected me by force. ... I ... respectfully ask the support of the General Government in my efforts to maintain rightful government of the State of Arkansas, and that the commander of the United States arsenal at this post be directed to sustain me in that direction. [Baxter to Grant, April 15, 1874]

†From: Edward McPherson, ed., *A Hand-Book of Politics for 1874* ... (Washington, D.C., 1874), pp. 87-100, 132.

Having been duly installed as Governor of Arkansas by the judgment of a court, I respectfully ask that the commanding officer at the arsenal be instructed to deliver the arms belonging to the State, now in his custody, or hold the same subject to my order. [Brooks to Grant, April 15, 1874]

I am instructed by the President to say, in answer to your dispatch to him of yesterday, . . . that he declines to comply with your request, as he is not advised that your right to hold the office of Governor has been fully and finally determined by the courts of Arkansas. [Williams to Brooks, April 16, 1874]

The President directs me to request that you will please instruct the commanding officer at Little Rock, Ark., to take no part in the political controversy in that State, unless it should be necessary to prevent bloodshed or collision of armed bodies. [O. E. Babcock, Secretary to W. W. Belknap, Secretary of War, April 16, 1874]

A few days since, in the absence of my counsel, and at a time wholly unexpected, the circuit judge of this county, . . . rendered judgment in favor of Brooks against me for the office of Governor of the State. . . . I was at once forcibly put out of the office. . . . All this was done, too, after the Supreme Court of this State had twice decided that no court in the State had jurisdiction of the case at all, and the Legislature alone had the jurisdiction. At once, on being ejected from the office, I took steps to restore myself, and to get possession of the office, and to carry on the government. The people are coming to my aid, and are ready to restore me at once. In making this organization, I am obstructed by the interference of the United States troops, in displacing my guards from the telegraph office; and now it is apprehended that there will be further interference. Such interference breaks me down, and prevents any effort on my part to restore the State government and to protect the people in their rights. I beg of you to modify any order to the extent of such interference, and leave me free to act in this way to restore law and peace as the legitimate Governor of the State. . . . I beg of you to remove the United States troops back to the arsenal, and permit me to restore the legitimate government by my own forces, which I will do promptly if the United States will not interfere. There is an armed insurrection against the legal State government here, and I call upon you to aid in suppressing it; but if you will not, then leave me free to act, and order the United States troops, without an hour's delay, to their own ground, and keep them out of my way. [Baxter to Grant, April 19, 1874]

I hereby inform you that one Elisha Baxter, a private citizen, pretending to be Governor of Arkansas, without warrant or authority of law, . . . called out armed bodies of men for the avowed purpose of attacking and capturing the capitol of the State by military force, and forcibly installing himself as Governor of such State. . . . Therefore I, Joseph Brooks, Governor of the

State of Arkansas, in pursuance of the Constitution and laws of the United States, hereby make application to your Excellency to protect the State capital and the State of Arkansas against domestic violence and insurrection. [Brooks to Grant, April 20, 1874]

I, Elisha Baxter, Governor of the State of Arkansas, beg leave to inform your excellency that divers evil-disposed persons, conspiring the overthrow of the government of the State of Arkansas, have unlawfully, and by force of arms, taken possession of the capitol building and archives of the government. . . .
Now, therefore, pursuant to the provision of the Constitution of the United States in that behalf, I respectfully call on your excellency for the necessary military force to suppress such insurrection and to protect the State against the domestic violence aforesaid. [Baxter to Grant, April 28, 1874]

Last evening Judges Bennett and Searle of the Supreme Court were arrested, and have been spirited away. . . . When asked what for, the officer replied that Baxter had reason to fear that the Supreme Court, if allowed to meet, might possibly pass upon some question that might prejudice his case now pending before the Attorney General of the United States, and that the court should not meet until the question of who is Governor should be decided at Washington. [Brooks to Grant, May 3, 1874]

Supreme Court decided to-day that the Pulaski circuit court has jurisdiction of the subject-matter of the case of Brooks *vs.* Baxter, and the judgment is regular and valid, and that I am Governor of Arkansas. [Brooks to Grant, May 7, 1874]

I was elected to the office of Governor of Arkansas by a large majority of the votes. This I have established by the proof. In the courts I have been adjudged entitled to the office by the circuit court, the only court of general jurisdiction in the State. . . . I am able to hold the situation against all the force the insurgents can rally, but prompt recognition and interposition on your part would prevent the effusion of much blood. [Brooks to Grant, May 9, 1874]

It is agreed this May 9, 1874, at Washington City, D.C., between the respective attorneys and agents of Joseph Brooks and Elisha Baxter, . . . that, . . . the Legislature of the State shall be called by the said Brooks and Baxter to meet in extra session on the fourth Monday of May, A.D. 1874, . . . they shall receive and entertain a communication from Mr. Brooks setting forth specifically the ground for his claim to the office of Governor, as well as his reasons for contesting Baxter's right thereto; that they shall investigate the facts and allegiations so set forth by Brooks, . . . the Legislature shall determine in the manner provided by law which of the contestants received, at the November election, 1872, a majority of the legal votes, and declare the result, and the parties shall abide that action. [Attorney General's Plan of Adjustment, Williams to Baxter and Brooks, May 9, 1874]

Your dispatch submitting proposition to submit question of who was duly elected Governor, ... as proposed in your dispatch, is accepted. [Brooks to Williams, May 10, 1874]

Yours of this date, submitting a proposition for the settlement of the troubles in Arkansas, is received and fully considered. ... I cannot consent to anything that will, in whole or part, recognize Brooks as Governor. I am Governor or I am not Governor. The Legislature has been called together for the 11th of this month. The members are rapidly assembling. ... The Legislature might as well meet now and act under my call [instead of as agreed in Washington], because it might not return two weeks hence, and in the meantime we are in confusion, with no recognized Governor and the State in war. ... If the Legislature meets now, the question may be submitted to it fairly, and I will abide its decision fully. I am therefore constrained to decline the terms proposed. [Baxter to Williams, May 9, 1874]

I am directed by the President to say that he considers your proposition fair and reasonable, and I have asked Mr. Brooks for its immediate adoption by him. [Williams to Baxter, May 11, 1874]

I recommend that the members of the General Assembly now at Little Rock adjourn for a reasonable time, say for ten days, to enable Brooks to call into the body his supposed adherents, so that there may be a full legislature. Any hasty action by a part of the Assembly will not be satisfactory to the people. [Grant to Baxter, May 11, 1874]

Hon. Elisha Baxter has telegraphed the President that the General Assembly must adjourn from day to day until a quorum is present, and that then he is in favor of its adjourning until every one of your supposed adherents is present. ... I am directed by the President to say that he considers this fair and reasonable, and your interests require its immediate acceptance. Answer. [Williams to Brooks, May 11, 1874]

This action I cannot and will not willingly submit to. Section one, article four, of the Constitution of the United States, declares that full faith and credit shall be given to the judicial proceedings of every State. ... I shall hold my troops together for the purpose of protecting the citizens of the State who believe the expression of the will of the people at the ballot-box should be enforced, and for the protection of those who stand by the Constitution, laws, and the adjudications of the courts of the country. ... It is time this agony, doubt, and uncertainty was over; the interests of humanity demand it shall be settled, and if you have the power under the Constitution and laws of the United States to settle the question of who is Governor of Arkansas adverse to the decision of the courts of the State, settle it, and settle it at once. ... I am confident that a legal quorum of the Legislature will not respond to Baxter's call, and I shall not assent nor be a party to convening the Legislature under any other agreement than that submitted by yourself through the Attorney General on the 9th instant. [Brooks to Grant, May 11, 1874]

The constitution of Arkansas, ... in my opinion, is decisive of this question as between Baxter and Brooks. According to the constitution and laws of the State, the votes for Governor were counted and Baxter was declared elected, and at once was duly inaugurated as Governor of the State. ... When it comes to decide a question of contest, the General Assembly is converted by the constitution into a judicial body, and its judgment upon that question is as final and conclusive as is the judgment of the Supreme Court of the State upon any matter within its jurisdiction. ... When the people of the State declared in their constitution that a contest about State officers *shall be determined* by the General Assembly, they cannot be understood as meaning that it might be determined in any circuit court of the State. ... Brooks appears to claim that when a contest for Governor is decided by the General Assembly, the defeated party may treat the decision as a nullity, and proceed *de novo* in the courts. This makes the constitutional provision as to the contest of no effect, and the proceedings under it an empty form. . . .

Looking at the subject in the light of the constitution alone, and it appears perfectly clear to my mind that the courts of the State have no right to try a contest about the office of Governor, but that exclusive jurisdiction over that question is vested in the General Assembly. . . .

On the 11th instant the General Assembly of the State was convened in extra session upon the call of Baxter, and both Houses passed a joint resolution pursuant to section 4 of article IV of the Constitution of the United States, calling upon the President to protect the State against domestic violence. This call exhausts all the means which the people of the State have, under the Constitution, to invoke the aid of the Executive of the United States for their protection, and there seems to be, under the circumstances of the case, an imperative necessity for immediate action. [Opinion of the Attorney General, Williams to Grant, May 15, 1874]

Whereas certain turbulent and disorderly persons pretending that Elisha Baxter, the present executive of Arkansas, was not elected, have combined together with force and arms to resist his authority as such executive, and other authorities of said State; and whereas said Elisha Baxter has been declared duly elected by the General Assembly of said State, as provided in the constitution thereof. . . .

Now, therefore, I, Ulysses S. Grant, President of the United States, do hereby make proclamation and command all turbulent and disorderly persons to disperse and retire peaceably to their respective abodes within ten days from this date, and hereafter to submit themselves to the lawful authority of said executive and the other constituted authorities of said State. ... [Presidential Proclamation Commanding the Dispersion of all Turbulent and Disorderly Persons in Arkansas, May 15, 1874]

19

"The Bloody Shirt"

In an emotional speech attacking the Ku Klux Klan on the floor of the House of Representatives in 1871, Representative Benjamin F. Butler dramatically held aloft the bloody shirt of a Mississippi school superintendent beaten by Klansmen earlier that year. The display made a sensation, and afterwards Republican speeches attacking Democrats for their role in the Civil War or in the suppression of black voters in the South were called "waving the bloody shirt." After the election setbacks of 1874, Republicans turned more and more to such speeches to maintain the enthusiasm of the faithful. Here is a stirring example by the finest practitioner of the art, Robert Green Ingersoll, believed to be one of the best orators of his day.

Document†
I am opposed to the Democratic party, and I will tell you why. Every state that seceded from the United States was a Democratic State. Every ordinance of secession that was drawn was drawn by a Democrat. Every man that endeavored to tear the old flag from the heaven that it enriches was a Democrat. Every man that tried to destroy this nation was a Democrat. Every enemy this great republic has had for twenty years has been a Democrat. Every man that shot Union soldiers was a Democrat. Every man that starved Union soldiers and refused them in the extremity of death a crust was a Democrat. Every man that loved slavery better than liberty was a Democrat. The man that assassinated Abraham Lincoln was a Democrat. Every man that sympathized with the assassin—every man glad that the noblest President ever elected was assassinated, was a Democrat. Every man that wanted the privilege of whipping another man to make him work for him for nothing and pay him with lashes on his naked back, was a Democrat. Every man that raised blood-hounds to pursue human beings was a Democrat. Every man that clutched from shrieking shuddering, crouching mothers, babes from their breasts, and sold them into slavery was a Democrat. . . . Soldiers, every scar you have got on your heroic bodies was given to you by a Democrat. Every scar, every arm that is lacking, every limb that is gone, every scar is a souvenir of a Democrat.

†From: Ingersoll, *The Works of Robert G. Ingersoll*, 12 vols. (N.Y.: Dresder Pub. Co., 1907), vol. 9, pp. 157-160.

20

The "Mississippi Plan"

Document 20-a†

The Election of 1875 in Mississippi

[In 1876 a congressional committee investigated the Mississippi election of the previous fall, the so-called Revolution of 1875. The Republican majority report describes the "Mississippi Plan." The Democratic minority report challenged the evidence and tried to minimize their allies' responsibility for the violence.]

(3.) Democratic clubs were organized in all parts of the State, and the able-bodied members were also organized generally into military companies and furnished with the best arms that could be procured in the country. The fact of their existence was no secret, although persons not in sympathy with the movement were excluded from membership. Indeed their object was more fully attained by public declarations of their organization in connection with the intention, everywhere expressed, that it was their purpose to carry the election at all hazards.

In many places these organizations possessed one or more pieces of artillery. These pieces of artillery were carried over the counties and discharged upon the roads in the neighborhood of republican meetings. . . . For many weeks before the election members of this military organization traversed the various counties, menacing the voters and discharging their guns by night as well as by day. . . .

(4.) It appears from the testimony that, for some time previous to the election, it was impossible, in a large number of the counties, to hold republican meetings. . . .

(5.) The riots at Vicksburgh on the 5th of July, and at Clinton on the 4th of September, were the results of a special purpose on the part of the democrats to break up the meetings of the republicans, to destroy the leaders, and to inaugurate an era of terror, not only in those counties, but throughout the State, which would deter republicans, and particularly the negroes, from organizing or attending meetings, and especially deter them from the free exercise of the right to vote on the day of the election. The results sought for were in a large degree attained.

†From: *Mississippi in 1875: Report of the Select Committee to Inquire into the Mississippi Election of 1875,* Senate Report No. 527, 44th Congress, 1st Session, pp. xiv-xv, xxv-xxvi, xxxvii-lxxxvii.

(6.) Following the riot at Clinton, the country for the next two days was scoured by detachments from these democratic military organizations over a circuit of many miles, and a large number of unoffending persons were killed. The number has never been ascertained correctly, but it may be estimated fairly as between thirty and fifty. . . .

(7.) The committee find . . . that the military organization extended to most of the counties in the State where the republicans were in the majority; that it embraced a proportion not much less than one-half of all the white voters, and that in the respective counties the men could be summoned by signals given by firing cannons or anvils; and that probably in less than a week the entire force of the State could be brought out under arms.

(8.) The committee find that in several of the counties the republican leaders were so overawed and intimidated, both white and black, that they were compelled to withdraw from the canvass those who had been nominated, and to substitute others who were named by the democratic leaders, and that finally they were compelled to vote for the ticket so nominated, under threats that their lives would be taken if they did not do it. . . .

(9.) The committee find that the candidates, in some instances, were compelled, by persecution or through fear of bodily harm, to withdraw their names from the ticket and even to unite themselves ostensibly with the democratic party. . . .

(10.) The committee find that on the day of the election, at several voting-places, armed men assembled, sometimes not organized and in other cases organized; that they controlled the elections, intimidated republican voters, and, in fine, deprived them of the opportunity to vote the republican ticket. [Majority report]

If the testimony touching the subjects within the scope of the resolution of the Senate could be reduced to such as is receivable under the rules of evidence, as recognized by courts of justice and by this Senate while sitting as a court, the testimony taken in Mississippi by this committee would be confined to a dozen pages of manuscript. The rest is rumor, hearsay, and opinion. . . .

A large body of these witnesses were negroes of the most ignorant and uncivilized description, who did not hesitate to state anything, and whose declarations were frequently of the wildest and most absurd character. . . .

Unfortunately the new and arbitrary political conditions imposed upon both races by the will of Congress were disturbed by the presence of a class of unscrupulous, needy, and rapacious adventurers who came down to fill the political offices. . . . The result was, as the testimony everywhere discloses, that the State and Federal offices to which any considerable emolument was attached fell into the hands of white men newly arrived within the borders of the State, ignorant and unsympathetic of the wishes and feelings of the white population, and bent wholly upon using the political material which they found ready at their hands in the shape of masses of ignorant, superstitious, and suspicious negroes to sustain themselves in office and power. Instead of encouraging the colored population to relations of amity and confidence with the whites who gave them employment and furnished them with the means of subsistence, it has been plainly the object and intent of these political adventurers to increase the distrust between the races, and to encourage on the part of the blacks and intensify the instinct and feeling of race opposition. In this, by means of low arts, they have been, unhappily, too successful, and the negroes of the State of Mississippi have been banded together in an unthinking mass, under the lead and blind control of a handful of northern strangers, with here and there a native white man. . . .

In 1875 . . . rumors flew thick and fast. The preparation of the governor and his arming of the negro militia were on every tongue, and caused the deepest distress and apprehension among all classes who sought to preserve the peace in the State and friendly relations between the two races. . . . The effect was to increase the insolence and insubordination of the blacks and intensify the discontent and the apprehensions of the whites. . . .

Thus opened the campaign of 1875. It is in proof, by almost every witness who was examined on the subject, that the negroes were organized in clubs, having a *quasi* military organization in every county in the State. Clubs, also, of white people were formed, and the parading and marching, with the use of flags, drums, music, cannon for salutes or the explosion of anvils, (a rude substitute for cannon,) became general throughout the State.

Much of the alleged intimidation of the colored people by the white population was claimed to be from causes like these, which could only have operated upon minds of the most childish character, and would be ridiculed if proposed, with the same intent, in any part of the Northern States. This constitutional timidity of the colored population was frequently and gravely urged as entering into alleged violations of the fifteenth amendment by white men, who fired off pistols in the air and exploded anvils at night on their return from meetings through the country. . . .

We deem it hardly necessary to make expression of the intense and hearty reprobation which we, in common with all men who respect and value law and order and humanity, necessarily felt, and now feel, upon every occasion where violence and crime were committed. Stern repression and prompt punishment are the just measures to be dealt out to all such offenders, without respect to race, or color, or station in life, and for all such criminals and transgressors we invoke due punishment at the hands of those who are the representatives of the Government whose laws need vindication. But while we propose in every proven case to condemn the guilty, we do not propose to allow reasonable proof to be replaced by reckless and malicious assertion or rumor; nor do we propose to condemn a whole community upon the testimony of men, confessedly without character, who live upon slanders and trade upon abuse, instigated, as many of such characters were who appeared before the committee, by a miserable faction, whose hope of prolonged plunder and self-enrichment lies in keeping up a condition of public excitement and fanning the prejudices and hatreds of illy-informed citizens of the North against the white people of the South. . . .

A condition of affairs which would be incredible and utterly intolerable in any of the Northern States exists in many of the black counties of Mississippi, where the property, intelligence, and character of the community is trodden to the earth, insulted, and ignored by the most ignorant and sometimes vicious members of the community. ... In such a condition of affairs, the forbearance and self-subordination exhibited by the white population demands and should receive the strong sympathy and high respect of every just and well-regulated mind. ... [Minority report]

Document 20-b†

The "Mississippi Plan" in South Carolina

[Compare the conclusion of the Democratic minority report above with this campaign plan South Carolina Democrats adopted from their Mississippi brethren.]

1. THAT EVERY Democrat in the Townships must be put upon the Roll of the Democratic Clubs. ...
2. That a Roster must be made of every white and of every Negro in the Townships and returned immediately to the County Executive Committee.
3. That the Democratic Military Clubs are to be armed with rifles and pistols and such other arms as they may command. They are to be divided into two companies, one of the old men, the other of the young men; an experienced captain or commander to be placed over each of them. ...
12. Every Democrat must feel honor bound to control the vote of at least one Negro, by intimidation, purchase, keeping him away or as each individual may determine, how he may best accomplish it.
13. We must attend every Radical meeting that we hear of whether they meet at night or in the day time. Democrats must go in as large numbers as they can get together, and well armed, behave at first with great courtesy and assure the ignorant Negroes that you mean them no harm and so soon as their leaders or speakers begin to speak and make false statements of facts, tell them then and there to their faces, that they are liars, thieves and rascals, and are only trying to mislead the ignorant Negroes and if you get a chance get upon the platform and address the Negroes.
14. In speeches to Negroes you must remember that argument has no effect upon them: they can only be influenced by their fears, superstitions and cupidity. Do not attempt to flatter and persuade them. ... Treat them so as to show them, you are the superior race, and that their natural position is that of subordination to the white man. ...
16. Never threaten a man individually. If he deserves to be threatened, the necessities of the times require that he should die. ...

†From: William A. Sheppard, *Red Shirts Remembered: Southern Brigadiers of the Reconstruction Period* (Atlanta: Ruralist Press, Inc., 1940), pp. 46-50.

29. Every club must be uniformed in a red shirt and they must be sure and wear it upon all public meetings and particularly on the day of election.

30. Secrecy should shroud all of our transactions. Let not your left hand know what your right hand does.

21 ═══════════

═══════════ # The Louisiana Crisis of 1877

In 1876 Louisiana again emerged with rival governments, the Republican one headed by S. B. Packard, and the Democratic one by Francis T. Nicholls. This time Grant did not even temporarily recognize either side's legitimacy, and when Hayes became president, he withdrew the federal troops separating the two sides.

Document†

The following concurrent resolution was this day adopted by the Legislature of the State of Louisiana in regular session convened:

"Whereas, The General Assembly is now in the annual session convened; and whereas certain evil disposed persons are forming combinations to disturb the public peace and defy the lawful authorities; and whereas the State is threatened with domestic violence; Therefore be it

"*Resolved*, ... That the President of the United States be requested to afford the protection guaranteed each State by the Constitution of the United States when threatened with domestic violence...." [Wm. P. Kellogg, Governor of the State of Louisiana to Grant, January 1, 1877]

Grave apprehensions felt that upon Nicholls' inauguration on Monday, he will forthwith appoint a Supreme Court, also a policeboard for this metropolitan district, assuming to be Governor. This board will supply a police force to capture the police-stations and dispute the beats. If this be done, it will be reënforced by the White League in strong force, pretending to be Nicholls' militia. The conflict thus precipitated may be avoided by prompt recognition on Monday of authority of incoming administration of Packard to be inaugurated that day, and if directions be given to General Augur to support it as the legal government. [Kellogg to Grant, January 5, 1877]

I am constrained to decline your request for the aid of troops to inaugurate the new State government to-morrow. To do so would be to recognize one of two rival governments for the State—executive and legislative—at the very time when a committee of each House of Congress is in the State capital of Louisiana investigating all the facts connected with the late election, at which each of the contestants claims to have been legally

†From: Edward McPherson, ed., *Hand-Book of Politics for 1878*, (Washington, D.C.: Solomons & Chapman, 1878), pp. 60-70.

elected. All the troops can be called upon to do will be to suppress violence if any should take place, and leave constitutional authority and means to settle which is the rightful Governor and which the legal Legislature. [Grant to Kellogg, January 7, 1877]

I have the honor to announce to you that I have this day been inaugurated Governor of the State of Louisiana, under the Constitution and laws thereof, and have entered upon the discharge of my duties as such. [Nicholls to Grant, January 8, 1877]

Having been declared by the Legislature of the State, as provided by the Constitution, duly elected Governor of Louisiana, I have this day taken the oath of office and entered upon the duties of the position. [Packard to Grant, January 8, 1877]

The State House is in a state of siege and environment by armed White League. Lieutenant Commander Kells, U.S. Navy, officially reports loud threats to shell or burn the State House tonight. The whole city is in terror. For God's sake act. Packard will hold State House till death. [J. R. G. Pitkin, U.S. Marshal, to Attorney General Alphonso Taft, January 9, 1877]

The armed bodies are the new police and armed posse, acting under order of the Nicholls government.
They have substantially possession of the city, except the State House. The arsenal and Supreme Court are reported to have surrendered to them.
I have declined to interfere on either side until there was a violent breach of the peace.
My orders simply authorize me to prevent violence and bloodshed. None has yet occurred. [Brigadier General C. C. Augur to J. D. Cameron, Secretary of War, January 9, 1877]

I have just received assurances from General Nicholls that the armed forces under his orders will be disbanded at once, and that he has given strict orders that no disturbances should occur. State House not disturbed. [Augur to Cameron, January 9, 1877]

Have just returned myself from State House. No mob about it, and no interruption to communication with it. Packard police on duty on street in front. A larger crowd than usual, perhaps, in streets about, but not the least disturbance. Packard applied for troops to assist sheriff in regaining possession of supreme court room. I declined, under my orders. [Augur to Cameron, January 10, 1877]

It has been the policy of the Administration to take no part in the settlement of the question of rightful government in the State of Louisiana, at least not until the Congressional Committees now there have made their report. But it is not proper to sit quietly by and see the State government gradually taken possession of by one of the claimants for Gubernatorial honors, by illegal means. The Supreme Court set up by Mr. Nicholls can receive no more recognition than any other equal number of lawyers convened on the call of any other citizen of the State. . . . A legal quorum of each house holding such certificates met and declared Mr. Packard Governor. Should there be a necessity for the recognition of either, it must be Packard. [Grant to Augur, January 14, 1877]

There seems, from what I can learn, a fixed determination on the part of a large majority of people here to resist in every possible way the establishment of the Packard government. They prefer a military one; in what manner and to what extent they will proceed cannot be told. I do not think murder and assassination are contemplated, certainly not by Nicholls. But they may result from such loose talk. Packard's opponents are numerous, united and aggressive, his friends few, unorganized, and furnish no moral or material support. From present appearances his government can only be maintained by use of United States troops. I do not understand that they care so much who is President. [Augur to the Adjutant General, U.S. Army, February 15, 1877]

Prior to my entering upon the duties of the Presidency there had been stationed by order of my predecessor in the immediate vicinity of the building used as a State House in New Orleans, Louisiana, and known as Mechanics' Institute, a detachment of United States infantry. Finding them in that place, I have thought proper to delay a decision of the question of their removal until I could determine whether the condition of affairs is now such as to either require or justify continued military intervention of the National Government in the affairs of the State.

In my opinion there does not now exist in Louisiana such domestic violence as is contemplated by the Constitution as the ground upon which the military power of the National Government may be invoked for the defense of the State. . . . Having the assurance that no resort to violence is contemplated, but on the contrary the disputes in question are to be settled by peaceful methods under and in accordance with law, I deem it proper to take action in accordance with the principles announced when I entered upon the duties of the Presidency.

You are therefore directed to see that the proper orders are issued for the removal of said troops at an early date from their present position to such regular barracks in the vicinity as may be selected for their occupation. [Hayes to George W. McCrary, Secretary of War, April 20, 1877]

On this day, the fifteenth anniversary of the surrender of New Orleans to the forces of the United States, it becomes my duty to announce to you that the aid and countenance of the National Government have been withdrawn from the Republicans of Louisiana, and that a government revolutionary in form is practically on the point of usurping the control of affairs in this State. . . .

I firmly believe that, had the legal government been recognized, it could have sustained itself without the intervention of troops; but the order for withdrawal, issued under the circumstances and in the manner it was issued, clearly indicated that even moral support, which the legal government of Louisiana should have received from the National administration, would be denied. Had the General Assembly continued in session at the State House, I should have deemed it my duty to have asserted and defended my government to the last, notwithstanding the withdrawal of troops; but with the Legislature disintegrated and no prospect of present success, I cannot task your tried fidelity by asking you longer to continue to aid me in the struggle I have thus far maintained. I therefore announce to you that I am compelled to abstain for the present from all active assertion of my government. I waive none of my legal rights, but yield only to superior force. I am wholly discouraged by the fact that, one by one, the Republican State Governments of the South have been forced to succumb to force, fraud, or policy. Louisiana, the first State rehabilitated after the war, is the last State whose government thus falls, and I believe it will be among the first to raise itself again to a plane of equal and honest representation. I advise you to maintain your party organization, and continue to battle for the rights of citizenship and free government. We strive for these, and not for man or men. It grieves me beyond expression that the heroic efforts you have made, and the cruel sufferings you have undergone to maintain Republican principles in Louisiana, have had this bitter end. To those who so gallantly stood by me in the long contest we passed through, I tender my heartfelt thanks. To all I counsel peace, patience, fortitude, and a firm trust that, eventually, right and justice will prevail. [Final address of Governor Packard to the Republican members of the State Legislature, April 25, 1877]

Part three

Bibliographic Essay

No era has occasioned more extreme swings in historical interpretation than that of American Reconstruction after the Civil War. For the best discussions of these changes in the historical literature, students should consult Larry Kincaid,"Victims of Circumstance: An Interpretation of Changing Attitudes Toward Republican Policy Makers and Reconstruction," *Journal of American History*, 57 (June 1970): 48-66, and Richard O. Curry, "The Civil War and Reconstruction, 1861-1877: A Critical Overview of Recent Trends and Intrepretations," *Civil War History*, 20 (September 1974): 215-38. The standard textbook on the era of the Civil War and Reconstruction is now James M. McPherson, *Ordeal by Fire: The Civil War and Reconstruction* (New York: Alfred A. Knopf, 1982).

The first scholarly assessments of Reconstruction appeared in the 1890s and the first decade of the twentieth century. Cited by white southerners to justify the formal disfranchisement and segregation of black southerners, William Archibald Dunning's *Essays on the Civil War and Reconstruction, and Related Topics* (New York: Macmillan Co., 1898); John W. Burgess's *Reconstruction and the Constitution, 1866-1876* (New York: Charles Scribner's Sons, 1902); and James Ford Rhodes's monumental *History of the United States from the Compromise of 1850 to the Final Restoration of Home Rule at the South in 1877*, 7 vols. (New York: Macmillan Co., 1893-1906) all confirmed southern charges that misguided or vindictive northern radical politicians had imposed cruel and often unconstitutional laws upon a devastated land and suffering people. This conviction was reinforced by a series of studies of individual southern states during Reconstruction, published primarily by Dunning's graduate students at Columbia University from 1900 to 1923. These histories unabashedly rested on "scientific" notions of black racial inferiority accepted by most white Americans at the turn of the century, and with rare exceptions portrayed the short term of Republican ascendancy in the South as an era of unparalleled corruption, venality, and incompetence in government. One of the exceptions was James Wilford Garner, *Reconstruction in Mississippi* (New York: Macmillan Co., 1901), which though relying primarily on Democratic sources of information credited at least some Republicans with sincerity. (Garner had the benefit of direct correspondence with Adelbert Ames, Mississippi's last Republican governor, who imparted to Garner a degree of skepticism of Democratic allegations.) Other less biased (though by no means *un*biased) works were William Watson Davis's account of *The Civil War and Reconstruction in Florida* (New York: Columbia University Press, 1913); Edwin C. Wooley, *The Reconstruction of Georgia* (New York: Columbia University Press, 1901); and C. Mildred Thompson, *Reconstruction in Georgia: Economic, Social, and Political, 1865-1872* (New York: Columbia University Press, 1915). Despite their shortcomings, some of the other state histories which appeared in these years remain the only books on the subject; they must be used with caution. They are Walter L. Fleming, *Civil War and Reconstruction in Alabama* (New York: Columbia University Press, 1905); Thomas S. Staples, *Reconstruction in Arkansas, 1862-1874* (New York: Columbia University Press, 1923); John R. Ficklin, *History of Reconstruction in Louisiana (Through 1868)* (Baltimore: John Hopkins University Press, 1910); Ella Lonn, *Reconstruction in Louisiana After 1868* (New York: G. P. Putnam's Sons, 1918); J. G. de Roulhac Hamilton, *Reconstruction in North Carolina* (New York: Columbia University Press, 1914); and John S. Reynolds, *Reconstruction in South Carolina, 1865-1877* (Columbia, S.C.: The State Co., 1905); Charles William Ramsdell, *Reconstruction in Texas* (New York: Columbia University Press, 1910); and Hamilton J. Eckenrode, *The Political History of Virginia During the Reconstruction* (Baltimore: Johns Hopkins University Press, 1904). The general American public learned of and accepted the pro-southern, anti-Republican version of Reconstruction history through Thomas Dixon, Jr.'s fictional romance of the Ku Klux Klan, *The Clansman* (New York: Doubleday, Page & Co., 1905), which reached an even wider audience in 1915 as part two of D. W. Griffith's epic film, *The Birth of a Nation.* In 1929 Claude G. Bowers's lively, nonfiction history of Reconstruction, *The Tragic Era: The Revolution After Lincoln* (Cambridge, Mass.: Houghton Mifflin & Co., 1929), reached the best-seller lists, succeeded by the most successful American novel of all time, Margaret Mitchell's *Gone With The Wind* (New York: Macmillan Co., 1936) and its brilliant movie version. The impact of these popular accounts on ordinary Americans was so great that many Americans still accept the view of Reconstruction they popularized, even after twenty-five years of unremitting attack by historians.

Howard K. Beale's *The Critical Year: A Study of Andrew Johnson and Reconstruction* (New York: Frederick Ungar Publishing Co., 1930) brought the perceptions of the Progressive historians to bear on the issues of the Reconstruction era. Sharing the Progressive historians' conviction that economic interests lay at the foundation of political controversies, Beale insisted that the Republican party really was the agent of northeastern capitalists during the Civil War era, and that its humanitarian appeals against slavery and racial oppression were merely subterfuges through which businessmen gulled northern voters into destroying the power of the anti-capitalist, agrarian South. Beale's revision of the old pro-southern interpretation of Reconstruction was quickly accepted by historians, who as a group generally shared his belief that economic interest determined human action. It was incorporated into James G. Randall's synthesis of the Civil War era, *The Civil War and Reconstruction* (Boston: D.C. Heath & Co., 1937), which in an edition revised by his eminent student, David Donald, long remained the standard text on its subject. In 1951 C. Vann Woodward seemed to confirm the economic interpretation, when he published the results of his investigation into the Compromise of 1877, which ended Republican efforts to control the state governments of the South. In *Reunion and Reaction: The Compromise of 1877 and the End of Reconstruction* (Boston: Little, Brown & Co., 1951), Woodward apparently demonstrated that the compromise consisted of far more that the bargain Paul Leland Haworth described in *The Hayes-Tilden Disputed Presidential Election of 1876* (Cleveland: Burrows Brothers Co., 1906). Rather than a mere agreement not to obstruct Republican Rutherford B. Hayes's formal election by the electoral college in exchange for his promise to end federal military interference on behalf of Republicans in the South, Woodward discovered in the negotiations of 1877 a broad agreement to unite northern and southern economic conservatives in the Republican party. While the political realignment failed to materialize, Woodward argued that the 1877 compromise marked the origin of the Republican-southern Democratic conservative coalition which opposed liberal legislation well into the 1950s and 1960s.

The 1930s also witnessed a growing challenge to the old portraits of the South during Reconstruction. Influenced by the axioms of Progressive history, Francis Butler Simkins and Robert Hilliard Woody offered a more sophisticated analysis of *South Carolina During Reconstruction* (Chapel Hill: University of North Carolina Press, 1932), acknowledging the progressivism of some Republican reforms and paying closer attention to economic issues in Reconstruction than their predecessors. Their effort was followed by Roger W. Shugg's *Origins of Class Struggle in Louisiana: A Social History of White Farmers and Laborers During Reconstruction and After* (University, La.: Louisiana State University Press, 1939), which viewed the Reconstruction controversy within the context of continuing struggles among local economic interests, and Horace Mann Bond's *Negro Education in Alabama: A Study in Cotton and Steel* (Washington: Associated Publishers, Inc., 1939), which remains the most stimulating and suggestive account of the relationship between Reconstruction politics and economic interests within the states. These studies, W.E.B. Du Bois's *Black Reconstruction: An Essay Toward a History of the Part which Black Folk Played in the Attempt to Reconstruct Democracy in America, 1860-1880* (New York: Harcourt, 1935), and Vernon L. Wharton's *The*

Negro in Mississippi, 1865-1890 (Chapel Hill: University of North Carolina Press, 1947), at the time still an unpublished doctoral dissertation, impelled Beale to call for a fundamental reevaluation of the entire Reconstruction era in a seminal article, "On Rewriting Reconstruction History," *American Historical Review,* 65 (July 1940): 807-27.

By the 1940s most historians were persuaded that Reconstruction in the South had not been so disruptive as once portrayed and that southern Republicans were something less than stone-hearted criminals and southern Democrats something more than suffering innocents. But the total rejection of the old stereotypes did not begin until the 1950s, as scientists debunked traditional ideas about racial inferiority and Americans were transfixed by an ever-accelerating civil rights movement. The greatest revolution occured in historical assessments of the early years of Reconstruction. Republicans emerged as men of humanitarian instincts, struggling against the accumulated prejudice of centuries. Important among these assessments were a series of studies that appeared in the 1960s–Eric L. McKitrick, *Andrew Johnson and Reconstruction* (Chicago: University of Chicago Press, 1960), which focused attention on the long-neglected moderate elements pf the Republican party; John Hope Franklin, *Reconstruction: After the Civil War* (Chicago: University of Chicago Press, 1961); William R. Brock, *An American Crisis: Congress and Reconstruction, 1865-1867* (New York: St. Martin's Press, 1963); LaWanda and John H. Cox, *Politics, Principle, and Prejudice, 1865-1866: Dilemma of Reconstruction America* (New York: Free Press of Glencoe, 1963); Kenneth M. Stampp, *The Era of Reconstruction, 1865-1877* (New York: Alfred A. Knopf, 1965); Hans L. Trefousse, *The Radical Republicans: Lincoln's Vanguard for Racial Justice* (New York: Alfred A. Knopf, 1968); and Michael Les Benedict, *A Compromise of Priciple: Congressional Republicans and Reconstruction, 1863-1869* (New York: W.W. Norton, 1975).

At the same time historians tested the Progressive historians' assumption that there was a link between northeastern capitalism and the Republican party, and they found that the evidence did not sustain it. Stanley Coben in "Northeastern Business and Radical Reconstruction: A Re-examination," *Mississippi Valley Historical Review,* 46 (June 1959): 67-90; Glenn M. Linden in " 'Radicals' and Economic Policies: The Senate, 1861-1873," *Journal of Southern History,* 32 (May 1966): 189-99 and " 'Radicals' and Economic Policies: The House of Representatives, 1861-1973," *Civil War History,* 13 (March 1967): 51-65; and Peter Kolchin in "The Business Press and Reconstruction, 1865-1868," *Journal of Southern History,* 33 (May 1967): 183-96, could find no Republican unity on economic issues, while Robert P. Sharkey argued that the more radical Republicans actually were economic liberals as well as racial egalitarians in *Money, Class, and Party: An Economic Study of the Civil War and Reconstruction,* (Baltimore: Johns Hopkins University Press, 1959).

Neo-revisionism (as the new interpretation of Reconstruction was often called) has had a powerful impact on historians' understanding of Reconstruction in the South itself. Michael Perman has studied southern reaction to the development of national Reconstruction policy in *Reunion Without Compromise: The South and Reconstruction, 1865-1868* (Cambridge, England: University Press, 1973) and *The Road to Redemption: Southern Politics, 1869-1879* (Chapel Hill: University of North Carolina Press, 1984). Allen W. Trelease and George C. Rabel have analyzed white violence against black and white Republicans in Trelease, *White Terror: The Ku Klux Klan Conspiracy and Southern Reconstruction* (New York and other cities: Harper & Row, 1971) and Rabel, *But There Was No Peace: The Role of Violence in the Politics of Reconstruction* (Athens, Ga.: University of Georgia Press, 1984). A series of books chronicling Reconstruction in individual southern states have replaced the old, Dunningite studies. Among the best are Elizabeth

Studley Nathans, *Losing the Peace: Georgia Republicans and Reconstruction, 1865-1871* (Baton Rouge: Louisiana State University Press, 1970); Jack P. Maddex, Jr., *The Virginia · Convervatives, 1867-1879: A Study in Reconstruction Politics* (Chapel Hill: University of North Carolina Press, 1970); William C. Harris, *The Day of the Carpetbagger: Republican Reconstruction in Mississippi* (Baton Rouge: Louisiana State University Press, 1979); Jerrell H. Shofner, *Nor Is It Over Yet: Florida in the Era of Reconstruction, 1863-1877* (Gainesville, Fla.: University Presses of Florida, 1974); Joe Gray Taylor, *Louisiana Reconstructed, 1863-1877* (Baton Rouge: Louisiana State University Press, 1974); and Ted Tunnell, *Crucible of Reconstruction: War, Radicalism and Race in Louisiana, 1862-1877* (Baton Rouge and London: Louisiana State University Press, 1984). All of these studies eschew the racism of the earlier works and describe southern Republicans as attempting to establish in the South the democratic and egalitarian priciples of the American heritage.

Neo-revisionists have also reassessed some special aspects of Reconstruction history. In his prize-winning *Reconstructing the Union: Theory and Policy During the Civil War* (Ithaca, N.Y.: Cornell University Press, 1969), Herman Belz has revised the anti-radical interpretations of Charles H. McCarthy, *Lincoln's Plan of Reconstruction* (New York: McClure, Phillips & Co., 1901); William Frank Zornow, *Lincoln & the Party Divided* (Norman: University of Oklahoma Press, 1954); and William B. Hesseltine, *Lincoln's Plan of Reconstruction* (Tuscaloosa, Ala.: Confederate Publishing Company, 1960). Michael Les Benedict's *The Impeachment and Trial of Andrew Johnson* (New York: W.W. Norton, 1973) challenged the conclusions of David Miller DeWitt's *The Impeachment and Trial of Andrew Johnson, Seventeenth President of the United States: A History* (New York and London: Macmillan Co., 1903), while Keith Ian Polokoff's *The Politics of Inertia: The Election of 1876 and the End of Reconstruction* (Baton Rouge: Louisiana State University Press, 1973) and Michael Les Benedict, "Southern Democrats in the Crisis of 1876-1877," *Journal of Southern History* 46 (November, 1980): 489-524 rebutted Woodward's *Reunion and Reaction*, already mentioned.

Overall, neo-revisionist historians of Reconstruction have stressed the general conservatism of both Republican Reconstruction legislation in Congress and Southern Republican programs in the South. Some, like William Gillette, *Retreat from Reconstruction, 1869-1879* (Baton Rouge and London: Louisiana State University Press, 1979), argued that Republicans' own racism prevented them from taking the bold measures necessary to radically transform the South. However, in recent years scholars have begun to stress once more how radical Reconstruction was, although they do not condemn that radicalism as the Dunningites did. In his *Nothing But Freedom: Emancipation and its Legacy* (Baton Rouge and London: Louisiana State University Press, 1983), Eric Foner has pointed out that in no other case of emancipation were freed slaves given a voice in the new arrangements that would replace slavery. Herman Belz points out that Reconstruction civil rights legislation was a radical departure from traditional American understandings of the federal system and civil rights, in his *A New Birth of Freedom: The Republican Party and Freedmen's Rights, 1861-1866* (Westport, Conn., and London: Greenwood Press, 1976).

Finally, in recent years there has been a revival of economic interpretations of the of the Reconstruction experience. Rejecting the old view of the Progressive historians that Republican Reconstruction was designed to secure the economic interests of northeastern capitalists, some historians still argue that Reconstruction reflected the ideology of early American capitalism. The course of Reconstruction, along with other events of the 1860s-1870s, brought out contradictions in that ideology which led to its fundamental alteration, with immense consequences for the whole country. For this interpretation, see David Montgomery, *Beyond*

Equality: Labor and the Radical Republicans, 1862-1872 (New York: Alfred A. Knopf, 1967); Eric Foner, *Politics and Ideology in the Age of the Civil War* (New York and Oxford, England: Oxford University Press, 1980); Foner, *Nothing But Freedom*, already noted; and Armstead L. Robinson, "Beyond the Realm of Social Consensus: New Meanings of Reconstruction for American History," *Journal of American History*, 64 (September 1981): 267-91.

This is by no means a complete review of the massive secondary literature on American Reconstruction after the Civil War. The student who wants to learn more must undertake what historians call a "literature search," a tedious job that will ultimately reward him or her with full understanding of this fascinating and exciting era.